Lean Ministry

Implementing Change in the 21st Century Church

By Charles M. Duffert
with
Dr. Jeffrey Hinds

Published by ChurchSmart Resources

We are an evangelical Christian publisher committed to producing excellent products at affordable prices to help church leaders accomplish effective ministry in the areas of Church planting, Church growth, Church renewal and Leadership development.

All Scripture quotations in this book are taken from the English Standard Version (ESV) copyrighted in 2001 by CrossWay Books.

For a free catalog of our resources call 1-800-253-4276.
Visit us at: www.ChurchSmart.com

Cover design by: Julie Becker
© Copyright 2011 by Charles M. Duffert

ISBN-13: 978-1-889638-96-6

Lean Ministry

Implementing Change in the 21st Century Church

Table of Contents

Remembering the warrior poet Charles Clifford McClain.
He was a man of principle.

FOREWORD

Common sense tells us that all results are the outcome of a process. But few people take the time to evaluate a process and then go to the trouble to improve it. Most people, even when displeased with the results, just take for granted that the process is what it is, and produces the results that its inherent capability allows. But if we look closely at processes, most of them are full of waste, do not flow very well, and are often interrupted by unanticipated or unplanned events.

Lean thinkers constantly evaluate and strive to improve processes. Their goal is continuous improvement. Many have described this akin to a religion, in which the individual is constantly wrestling with improving not only his or her own life, but also the lives of those around him or her. James Womack, chairman and founder of the Lean Enterprise Institute, has a mantra: "If the process is right, the results will be right."

So why not look at the individual process steps and their flow, and solve the problems that are preventing the process from producing improved results? This type of problem solving is, in fact, the definition of continuous improvement.

Christianity is such a process and has been in place for twenty centuries. In fact, we have many methods, or processes, for spreading the gospel and transforming individual lives by introducing them to the grace provided only by Christ Himself. On earth, Jesus Christ was the ultimate example of a "process in the flesh": walking, teaching, and giving his flesh and blood on the cross. The cross was a sacrificial step that provided the justification for our salvation. One way to describe a Christian's walk with Christ is by process steps: *justification* provided on the cross, *sanctification* as we walk and live every day, and *glorification* when we meet our Creator. Today that same process lives on in the person of the Holy Spirit of Jesus.

Can we improve our methods to introduce more people to Christ and assist them in their everyday walk? Is the twenty-first-century church up to the task? Can the church's contribution to the transformation process be improved? At the Lean Enterprise Institute, and at many other high-performing organizations, we believe that all processes can be improved—and that it is every individual's responsibility in that organization to work on this improvement.

There are proven methodologies for evaluating and improving processes, and therefore expanding good results. From our experience at the Lean Enterprise Institute, more than 90% of mature organizations intending to improve quality, reduce cost, and better employ limited resources use these methodologies. I was delighted to see the work of Don Pope, Andrew Parris, and Kent Smith in *Christianity Today—"The Lean Church, Streamlining Your Ministry for Maximum Effectiveness"*—as they evaluated and offered ideas to improve Christian outreach using the resources available in the local church.

Charles Duffert has provided an extensive, enjoyable, and practical perspective on improvements for the twenty-first-century church. He keeps Christ and what the Bible says about our world first while offering fair evaluation and very practical and proven ideas for improvement of the use of the resources that are available to church leaders. The evangelical community seldom receives constructive input of this caliber from its constituency. We have examples of good Lean practice in practically every industry, including health care and government services. Womack has also said, "No one who has tried to create a complete Lean improvement with the hands-on participation of top management has failed to achieve dramatic results." This is a very powerful statement about organizational improvement, and it applies to the evangelical community as well as the secular.

I encourage you to absorb what Charles has to offer in this important work. Please apply his ideas and let him know if you get improved results. Then strive to improve those results again—and again.

Dave Logozzo
President, Lean Enterprise Partners
Lean Enterprise Institute
Cambridge, MA
June 2010

INTRODUCTION

"Ya take what ya need and ya leave the rest..."
"The Night They Drove Old Dixie Down"
Robbie Robertson, 1969

So, why write a book about Lean thinking? Better yet, from your perspective, why read a book about Lean thinking while thinking about your ministry? Because Lean could prove to be very valuable to your work. The value of Lean is that it defines the intended outcome in specific terms and then progressively eliminates actions and processes that do not achieve the desired result. Lean thinking is all about getting at, and then fixing, the real problem—permanently! It is not about fixing the symptoms, nor about hiding problems with layers of non-value-adding activities and unnecessary costs. Lean thinking engenders the relentless pursuit and elimination of waste, however that waste manifests itself.

Why are we so concerned about waste in the church since there's no profit motive? Businesses must maximize value and minimize waste if they hope to match finite resources to infinite needs and respond to their customers' requests. Ministry is about being used by God to save the lost; it has eternal consequences (2 Corinthians 5:20). And if you're in ministry you know a thing or two about finite resources and infinite needs. So, in ministry, how much more important is it to minimize waste and maximize value?

We have struggled to walk a fine line between critique and criticism and have done our best to put ourselves second and to put Christ and what the Bible says about our world first. This book offers a few challenges to consider about the attitudes, behaviors, and paradigms of some within the twenty-first-century church. This could sting, and it could rankle some, although neither is our intent. Keep in mind that we are profiling the church-at-large, and its general characteristics, and not the detailed characteristics of specific denominations or local churches. Also, let us keep in mind that our business has eternal significance, so enduring a bit of pain in order to improve ministry is well worth it.

The most difficult part has been to communicate the need for change without implying that the church is broken, or that it needs to be scrapped and rebuilt. The church is not broken, but we can all certainly agree that the church needs to change and adapt to more effectively minister to the people who are its future—our youth—who have become a series of postmodern generations. Ultimate truth, rational thought, and a commonly understood system of values have tragically taken a backseat in our culture—and to some degree in the church.

As you read this book, all of it will appeal to some of you, and some of it will appeal to all of you. It is doubtful that all of it will appeal to all of you. Some readers will draw the wrong conclusion that we recommend running a church like a business. This is not the case—a church is not a business. This is not another book on how to run a church like a business. In fact, the opposite is most often true. As you read through this book we hope you will agree with us when we say *successful businesses are generally run like successful churches.*

The church is a God-given organization, the Bride of Christ (Ephesians 5), and exists to fulfill God's desires. Though it is not a business, like all organizations, the church has a mission, raw materials, structured processes, and people who execute those processes. Also, like other organizations, the church has value-adding activities and non-value-adding activities. To meet the needs of a changing postmodern world, the church must change as well. God's Word is the plumb line for our day-to-day living and needs no changing, but we can and should improve our human stewardship of ministry processes. This change must not compromise the essence of what we are teaching and living (Galatians 1:6-10), but we must be willing to change some of our methods (1 Corinthians 9:24-27). The essence of the gospel is timeless; it is applicable to all generations in all places. It is truth and must remain so—it is the only constant we have (John 17:17). But the twenty-first-century church has not adapted at the same rate as the world around it. This provides a conundrum as to how the local church can expect to meet the needs of a changing world without watering down the gospel or presenting a dumbed-down version of God.

The Bride of Christ will continue to grow beautiful. God will continue to prepare her until the day of the wedding feast (Matthew 26:29). His ends will not be thwarted. But what about the individual churches comprising the Bride? They face a choice to be more or less relevant to the world around them. Those that seek to be more relevant will flourish with the Bride. Those that do not will wither and sometimes perish as we see in the seven examples of Revelation 2–3. If we do not steward what God has given us, to directly serve His desires, there is simply no reason for our existence.

It is incumbent upon the senior stewards in our local churches to know the difference between what works and what doesn't work to meet the transformation needs of the people groups which God has led across their paths. They are accountable not to engage in wasteful activities, programs, or policies and to maintain the purity of the gospel at the same time. It is thus that they must lead, both inside and outside the walls of the local church. All churches are composed of people with various gifts and skills. Many of them have the skill of problem solving and understand that improvement methodologies are necessary. We do not want to waste the talents and skills of our church body and miss out on results that can be realized in our ministry.

There is a significant body of knowledge available in print on the subject of church development and church planting. These books talk about simple churches, cell churches, purpose-driven churches, and organic systems, among other models. They profile specific churches that have either fulfilled their mission or not. They present detailed analyses of what this or that church did resulting in this or that success or failure. This is good if your church is exactly like this or that church. But your church is unique. It is a special collection of people with a corporate personality like none other. It may be similar, but it's not the same. If you hope to make your church more effective at ministry, you have three choices. First, you can try to adapt and apply whatever the other guys did. This is a common practice that fails to recognize that every culture is unique, all leaders are created unique, and one's church may well implode by blindly stealing what worked for the other guys without recognizing the unique composition of every church and community. Second, you can start from scratch, re-create the wheel, and implement changes using the trial and error method. Both options are clumsy, fraught with danger, and ineffective. We believe there is a third choice—Lean ministry.

Lean thinking focuses on getting results by eliminating waste and looks outside the organization for direction on how and when to change its processes without compromising the quality of the results. With Lean, we can improve quality and reduce cost while making our members' efforts more organized and more fruitful. The acid test of Lean ministry is that it must be more productive, less costly, and it must create a more harmonious environment in which to live and it must never compromise quality. If we don't meet these three criteria, we have failed at our Lean transformation. Successful Lean implementation always results in a win-win situation for all members whether inside or outside the organization. Remember, God is the Master of the win-win situation.

More churches than we would like to admit are deeply mired in wasteful and ineffective activities, attempting vainly to draw people to them, rather than thinking and reaching outside self-imposed boundaries. We recognize there are evolving forms of the present-day church, some of which are not burdened with excessive waste. These are often churches that have been born of a particular need to minister to some splinter element of postmodern culture. Often they are not churches within mainline denominations. In cases where these churches have compromised the essence of truth, many have withered and died. God does not compromise.

This book is written first for denominational and senior leaders of twenty-first-century evangelical churches. It will most benefit those who lead churches with a central location, a well-established congregation led by an educated, professional cadre, and some form of structured government. It is secondarily written for any church or para-church organization, be it large or small, having Christ as the center of its ministry and demonstrating evangelicalism by wishing to grow that ministry to reach out and spread the gospel to the changing world around it.

To serve its purpose, a book, like a person, must have a clear and honest understanding of what it is. To best know what it is, it must know what it is not. This book is neither complicated, nor a high academic work, nor a comprehensive statement of theology. It does make pointed statements about selected elements of theology and recommends how the twenty-first-century church might respond to them. This is not an exhaustive analysis of every problem facing the church today. It simply suggests a focused way of looking at what is important to Him whom we serve. In Richard Pascale's book, *Delivering Results*, he says, "We are all much more likely to act our way into a new way of thinking than to think our way into a different way of acting."

Our Lord has very specific standards for the Bride of Christ. Today's church needs to stand alone as a unique beacon of His glory in a postmodern world; it can only do this if it will shed its accumulated waste.

We believe this book can serve a constructive purpose in the lives of everyday practitioners of Christian ministry even though it does not claim to be the complete answer to anyone's ministerial needs. It explains how we can use what we have to achieve the greatest impact in our attempt to meet the spiritual needs of a changing world. The book's thesis is simple and will be repeated in many ways throughout the following pages. It is this:

All organizations, be they secular or parochial share common characteristics. Each exists to meet someone's needs or to serve someone's desires—that person or persons being the end-user. These organizations all have raw material, processes that transform that raw material, and all use people to steward those processes. There are quality specifications determined by the end-user for whatever those processes produce. Within those processes there are value-adding activities and non-value-adding activities. Anything those organizations do or anything they have that does not contribute to the usefulness or the value of the product is wasteful. For organizations to increase the usefulness of the product for the end-user they must minimize the quotient of waste within all that they do. Waste is the enemy of value and Lean is the enemy of waste. Lean minimizes waste and increases value. Implementing Lean will minimize waste in all organizations. A church is an organization and Christianity is a process stewarded by people and has quality specifications determined by the End-User. The church can use Lean to make its process and people more effective just like any other organization.

Lean thinking focuses the energies of the entire organization on meeting the needs of the end-user—the external customer. In the case of Christianity, God is the recipient of all we do (Matthew 22:37-38). God certainly does have desires, such as His glory and fame being spread (Romans 11:36), our obedience and maturity (Colossians 1:28-9), and that all would come to know His Son as Savior (John 3:16). But God is not a *customer* because He has no needs.

Since God has no needs, there can be no fair exchange of goods and services or payment-in-kind between us and Him. Yet we serve Him, even though He is the initiator as well as the receiver of everything. He is our Lord and the sole reason for our existence. He defines what is important and what is not—what is valuable and what is waste. Our Triune God's greatest value is His own glory and His glory is most clearly manifested in the transformation of those whom He has called unto Himself into the likeness of His Son, Jesus Christ.

The raw material for this transformation process is the spiritual DNA that we all receive at the moment of conversion (Philippians 1:6). This spiritual DNA, common to all believers, passes through an incremental transformation process on a timeline unique to each individual believer. The transformation process will nurture and grow our spiritual DNA, but it will proceed depending on several factors, including our Lord's timing, the submission of the believer, and the support of the community—that is, the local church.

To be effective and efficient, the transformation process will take place in an environment formatted to fit the culture and social characteristics of the people group being transformed (1 Corinthians 9:19-23). But cultural and social sensitivities must never compromise the essence of God's nature, the truth of what He has spoken, or the spiritual DNA of the believer. The church's mission is to make itself available as the venue in which the transformation process can take place (Colossians 1:27-28). The Spirit of God provides the impetus for the individual to grow by exerting a constant pull on that believer to move forward and flow through the transformation process (Galatians 5:22-23). The church's role is to provide the opportunity for the believer to flow through the transformation process in response to the Holy Spirit's pull. To provide optimum flow for the believer, the local church must engage in an absolute minimum of programs, policies, and activities not contributing directly to the transformation of the believer. To do this, the local church must execute its mission with a minimum of waste. Moreover, it must seek input from its constituency to effectively execute its mission, adapt to changing internal and external conditions and stimuli, and continuously eliminate wasteful activities. This is done by using small cross-functional teams with specific foci to ensure the local church fulfills its mission as an organ of transformation (Acts 6:1-7).

Whatever we have as our product, process, or customer, in a world of limited time and space, we must minimize the consumption of our resources by minimizing wasteful, non-value-adding activities. Our customer defines value; those producing the product do not. Because of this, the believing church has a huge advantage, because Christ has already defined the value and set His people on a mission. The organization producing the product must respond to customer requirements by providing that value. This should be self-evident, but many organizations miss this fundamental point. It is the organization's job to supply value to the customer, supply it when it is required, and supply it in the amount that it is required. This is the sole reason for the existence of any organization with a product, including churches. If it cannot do this, it has no purpose.

This book is a blueprint to help eliminate waste in ministry. It can help guide the reader to what will work for his or her ministry. It is a template to help us discern how our Lord is asking us to work with Him to achieve His ends. At the very least it tells us what we must do to get out of His way so He can work. It is written from both sides of the pulpit—one side represented by a career professional change agent and the other side represented by a career pastor. Both careers have been spent in the reality of trench warfare in the lives of real people. Trench warfare is tedious and ugly. Making change is difficult. It is our fervent hope that you, the Reader, can use these simple concepts to make your ministry more effective for our Lord.

Chapter 1

Why Toyota Matters to You

"Sometimes the light's all shinin' on me;
Other times, I can barely see.
Lately it occurs to me . . .
What a long, strange trip it's been."
"Truckin"
– The Grateful Dead, 1970

Toyota probably doesn't matter much to you unless you are a Toyota employee or you drive one of their vehicles. If you are a disciple of Jesus Christ, or if you are involved in any way in the transformation of disciples, what could matter very much to you is how Toyota accomplished some truly great things by using what we now call Lean Enterprise.

Lean Enterprise has gained enormous popularity in the U.S. because it guarantees product quality improvement and cost reduction. You could easily read this book and draw the wrong conclusion that we are trying to apply business principles in a spiritual context. Exactly the opposite is true. We believe that what we now call Lean is the application of principles that God hardwired into creation from the beginning—it just hasn't been used in ministry for a long time.

The Bible is our basis for making that last statement. God is intentional, rational, and focused, and He's not about wasting the resources that He created to satisfy His goals. Of course, the Bible doesn't talk about "Lean Enterprise," but examples abound from the first book to the last. Our Lord intends to get results, and results are got by minimizing waste. We believe these methodologies were applied in Jesus' ministry and in the first-century church, as well as in successful ministries throughout history. Jesus, His original disciples, and the early church did what was necessary—but only what was necessary—to accomplish God's charter to them. Why only what was necessary? Because to do anything more would have been resources wasted, misspent on nonproductive activities.

Jesus was Lean. His disciples were Lean. The first-century church was Lean. By being Lean, the early church accomplished phenomenal things. In *The Forgotten Ways*, Alan Hirsch postulates that at the end of the first century AD there were 20,000 Christians in the world. But by the end of the third century AD that number had grown to 25,000,000. That's progress! Nothing we have done since then has rivaled the effectiveness of the first-century church. Nearly twenty centuries later, if we hope to match that sort of progress, we need to identify and examine commonalities between then and now.

Before we draw parallels to Christian ministry we need to explain how Lean Enterprise works. We will start with a practical example of Lean's success which we can all understand. A discussion of the reconstruction of the Japanese economy and the revival of Toyota Motor Works, Ltd. subsequent to World War II is our starting point. This chapter may seem like teaching Greek by speaking Greek. But it's important for you to understand where Lean Enterprise came from and why it works no matter which product, process, customer, or venue to which it is applied. In the next chapter we will get down to the nuts and bolts of Lean principles, introduce some new terms, and begin to explore how the church can apply Lean principles to eliminate waste and more effectively communicate the gospel to a world in need.

The World War II Multimedia Database estimates total Japanese military casualties during World War II to be 1.3 million dead and 4 million wounded or missing. Total civilian casualties were 672,000 dead with 1.5 million wounded or missing. The toll was so great that some sources do not distinguish between military and civilian casualties. About 3% of Japan's pre-war population was killed. To put it in more personal terms, if it were in today's United States; an unthinkable 9 million people would perish.

Much print area has been devoted to the atomic bombing of Hiroshima and Nagasaki. But that was only part of the damage. The atomic bombs dropped on those cities were simply the coda to a symphony of destruction resulting in a nearly desolate nation. The U.S. War Department's *Strategic Bombing Survey—Pacific War—1 July 1946* tells us that 30% of the Japanese population lost their homes. Sixty-six Japanese cities were at least 40% destroyed by United States bombing raids. Thirty-one square miles in the cities of Tokyo, Kobe, Nagoya, and Osaka were destroyed. Tokyo was bombed fourteen times. By July 1, 1945, in less than one year, overall industrial output was down to 40% of its peak in 1944.

At the end of World War II the Japanese economy was destitute and the country's infrastructure was largely reduced to rubble. Heretofore successful companies had become dysfunctional and bankrupt. Among them was Toyota, which was reduced to a shadow of its wartime self.

Japan's unconditional surrender at the end of World War II permitted a unique intervention on the part of the victor nations. An Allied Occupation Force instituted sweeping political, social, and economic reforms between the years of 1945 and 1952 to democratize the country against the rising tide of communism and to minimize a resurgence of Japanese militarism during reconstruction. A by-product of this occupation was to reconstruct the Japanese economy to some level of self-sufficiency.

One method used by the Allied Occupation Force to stabilize the economy was to restrict credit, intending to fix it in place as a baseline for reconstruction. As a result, Toyota couldn't borrow money to buy capital equipment. Also, because large-scale unemployment would further destabilize the economy, the Allies would not allow Toyota large-scale workforce layoffs to save money and start over. In time, Toyota was allowed to lay off one-third of its employees, but the remaining two-thirds were guaranteed employment for life—a commitment of honor that Toyota fulfilled even in the absence of a legally binding contract.

Pascal Dennis tells us in *Lean Production Simplified* that it was under these impossible conditions that Toyota Motor Works, Ltd. intended to compete in a world market. One could not script a worse situation. It was not pretty but compete they did. Between 1945 and 1950 Toyota produced a total of only 2,650 motor vehicles. By comparison, in 1950, Ford Motor Company was producing 7,000 motor vehicles per day.

We don't want to focus on Toyota—the book is about Christian transformation. But there is no better twentieth or twenty-first century example of the effectiveness of Lean than Toyota's.

Toyota Motor Company had humble beginnings starting in 1933 when its parent company, Toyoda Automatic Loom, created a new division to produce passenger automobiles. During World War II, the company was dedicated to producing trucks for the Japanese Imperial Army. Wartime material shortages required these vehicles be designed and produced quickly and simply.

After the War, Dr. W. Edwards Deming, an inconspicuous statistician, educator, and consultant, was pivotal in the reconstruction of the Japanese economy in general and in particular with Toyota Motor Corporation. Dr. Deming's profound, yet simple, success strategies offered ways to achieve lasting growth and success. Dr. Deming is still largely unknown in this country but is regarded as the single most important person contributing to the reconstruction of the Japanese economy after World War II. He is a national hero in that country and each year the Deming Prize is awarded for manufacturing excellence in Japan—this being equivalent to a Nobel Prize in manufacturing.

Without going into the intermediate details, suffice it to say that Toyota has become very successful using simple improvement techniques. In 2005, Toyota was the 4th largest auto company in the world. In 2006 it surpassed Chrysler and Ford to become number two. In 2008, Toyota became the largest automobile manufacturer in the world, eclipsing the Big Three U.S. automakers. This having been accomplished prior to the economic downturn in 2008. Today, Forbes lists Toyota as the world's third largest company with revenues exceeding $256 billion and more than 324,000 employees and manufacturing or assembly plants in twenty countries.

What evolved between 1950 and today is called the Toyota Production System; renamed Lean Manufacturing in 1990 and most recently has been called Lean Enterprise. Lean principles are being applied universally to manufacturing, business, healthcare, education—and, the transformation process.

One could draw a cheap conclusion from Toyota's recent negative press due to vehicle recalls that Lean doesn't work. But the fact that organizations suffer serious problems from time to time doesn't negate the standard by which they operate or the goals they attempt to achieve. If this were the case, every church that experienced problems would render Christ and Christianity as flawed, broken, and ineffective. Neither does Toyota's present difficulty reflect negatively on the standards and processes they used to build a financial empire from the ashes of post-War Japan. Toyota will do what they have done since the end of World War II—use Lean principles to help them rebound from their recent recall difficulties.

Toyota's success is not solely due to business or financial management genius. Certainly, they've used solid business and financial principles. But their success is more directly related to the application of some non-business rules that have their roots in a more generic and comprehensive context that long predates Toyota. These improvement methodologies have been found, are found, and will continue to be found in successful organizations regardless of the product and market—and have since been validated by top business programs such as MIT

Sloan School of Management, Kellogg School of Management, Wharton, and Harvard Business School, among others.

What we now call Lean is not completely rooted in Japan. Henry Ford had successfully implemented Lean-type efficiencies in automobile manufacturing between the years 1910 and 1926. United States industrial production during World War II used similar methodologies to out-supply our enemies. Toyota creatively used what we now call the Toyota Production System, or Lean, to maximize their limited capital and labor resources to ensure their survival. In the thirty years following World War II they established themselves as a manufacturing entity to be reckoned with. Toyota simply assembled them into a template that's easy to understand and to use.

The Toyota Production System focuses on the pursuit and elimination of waste within existing processes and systems instead of simply adding people, capital equipment, and larger factories. In 1990, the Toyota Production System became known worldwide as Lean Manufacturing through the book *The Machine That Changed the World* by James Womack and Daniel Jones. Lean Manufacturing has been so successful in the companies using it that it is now being applied in service and health care businesses. Dr. Womack recently stated, "We now have examples of good Lean practice in practically every industry, even including government services. No one who has tried to create a complete Lean Enterprise with the hands-on participation of top management has failed to achieve dramatic results."

The challenges facing Toyota in 1945 were not unlike the challenges facing the church today. To survive after World War II, Toyota used Deming's methods to augment their own creativity. When comparing the present-day church to post-World War Two Japanese reconstruction, we acknowledge that the church is not destroyed. It is, more or less, intact. But it is not as healthy as it should be, and it is burdened with wasteful activities. The challenge the church faces today is no less critical than the challenge faced by Japan in 1945. Many churches doggedly continue as if there is no problem—much like Emperor Hirohito did until he personally toured the destruction of his homeland in 1945. Then it became personal. Then he felt the pain. It is time for the church to take the challenges personally and to feel the pain. God will not let His Bride languish and wither. But, neither can she be in the full radiance of her beauty when we continue to do things that do not work as He had intended.

The Toyota Production System was born of a need to overcome adversity so great as to be virtually not understandable by today's standards. Toyota didn't have much to start over with in 1945 but they accomplished great things in a short period of time against all odds. Their only choice was to make do with what they had and systematically eliminate waste from their existing systems using what we have learned to call Lean Enterprise. They went from near ruin to a towering giant in their community in fifty short years. Toyota did not have a business quarter without profit until the worldwide economic slide in 2008.

The church, too, can adapt to and meet the needs of a world having changed exponentially in recent years without compromising our Lord or His truth. The church will accomplish this not by garnering more financial, physical, and other sophisticated resources. She can do it through the focused and deliberate application of the principles and methods of Lean Enterprise in a spiritual context.

Chapter 2

What is Lean?

"I'm flying in Winchester cathedral.
All religion has to have its day
Expressions on the face of the Saviour
Made me say…I can't stay.
Open up the gates of the church and let me out of here!
Too many people have lied in the name of Christ
For anyone to heed the call.
So many people have died in the name of Christ
That I can't believe it all."
"Cathedral"
– Graham Nash, 1977

Lean Enterprise generates dramatic improvements in organizations wishing to improve the quality of their product and to reduce cost at the same time. To start, Lean classifies any activity within any organization as either value-added or non-value-added and then defines all non-value-added activities as waste. Value is what the customer wants. Remember, waste is the enemy of value, and Lean is the enemy of waste.

Value is added for our customer when we change something from raw material into something that meets our customer's needs. Non-value-adding activities are all those things we are required to do to get the work done, the way we do our work or the limitations of our work processes—many of them self-imposed.

Value stream measurements often show that organizations which do not use Lean find that less than 5% of their total expended resources actually add value. The remaining 95% is non-value-added activity, or waste. It seems incredible, but many profitable organizations sometimes have only 2-3% value added to their product.

The brilliance of Lean is that it progressively distills elements and activities common to any organization or any people group into actions that will improve the performance of even the most unique, sophisticated, or esoteric organization. This is not done in some sort of free-for-all environment; rather, there is a well-defined structure in which specific tools are used to produce results.

We must listen to and really hear what the customer has to say about our product. The customer specifies quality and delivery expectations, demand schedules, and whether we are meeting expectations. Lean depends on continually monitoring the voice of the customer. We can't just check in at long intervals and expect to have quality feedback on what the customer expects of us. This is what Lean calls the voice of the customer or VOC. We must listen to the VOC in order to continuously monitor that relationship and to respond quickly and constructively.

Lean tools: make the processes perform reliably and dependably; organize and standardize the workplace; simply measure performance; visibly publish or post performance so all can see it; and, foster a culture of continuous improvement involving all persons involved.

The Five Principles of Lean

Once we know and are listening to our customer, Lean is implemented using five fundamental principles to pursue and eliminate seven categorical forms of waste. This waste is common to any organization and degrades its ability to provide value to its customers, stay profitable, and compete in complex markets. We will introduce and explore these seven forms of waste and draw parallels to Christian ministry later in the book. When implemented in a culture of continuous improvement that involves all members of the organization, Lean results in accelerated processing speed, improved quality, and reduced cost for customers, employers, and employees alike. The five principles of Lean are shown below.

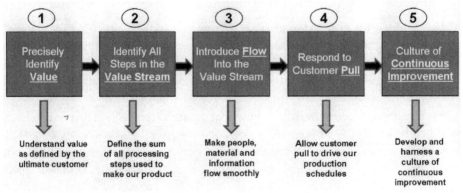

Figure 2.1: The Five Principles of Lean

Value

The starting point for Lean thinking is to understand what is valuable from the viewpoint of our customer—our end user—who is the reason for our existence. As we mentioned earlier, value is created when something that the customer needs is created or improved. To do this, we must know our customer—we cannot just know about the customer—hence the importance of listening to the VOC, discussed earlier. When we know our customer intimately, we will know what the customer defines as value. Value is the only thing that matters to the customer. Many organizations have a tendency to use technology, expensive assets, and employ our personal biases simply because we have them; often we simply do. Sometimes they do things a certain way because that is the way it's always been done or because that's the way the other guy is doing it. We need to put these notions aside and rethink the entire process from the customer's viewpoint.

To use a manufacturing example, cutting, milling, and polishing a piece of steel bar stock into a hydraulic cylinder all add value for the customer. What does not add value is all the time that piece of steel waits between operations or moves long distances around the factory. No value is added by putting it in inventory and counting it and then retrieving it for the next operation. The machine operator may spend long periods of wasted time waiting for work to arrive. While he or she is waiting we may set them to work on something that we don't really need just to keep them busy. Or he or she may have to repair defective work or scrap it out and make it again. All of this is non-value-added activity, or cost, for which the customer will not pay. The manufacturer absorbs these costs. We have the freedom to use our resources as we wish. But if all of our activities are either value-added or non-value-added, we must acknowledge the customer wants only value. Cost consumes the use of our limited resources that could and should be used to provide value.

Value Stream

Lean looks at something called the value stream to understand and quantify if we are providing value to our customer. The value stream is the sum of all processing steps used to make whatever it is that we are producing, including all value-added and non-value-added activities. This product could be an automobile, or it could be paper products, or bakers' flour. It could be an insurance payment or a hospital patient undergoing a medical treatment. Or, it could be a disciple being transformed into the likeness of Jesus Christ. Understanding the characteristics of the value stream is paramount because the value stream is the basis for any improvement initiative and the elimination of waste.

Flow

When we clearly understand our customer's values and our value stream, we must eliminate waste in our processes to make the value-generating steps flow. Whatever we produce should flow without impediment from the start of the process to the end of the process. To minimize the cost of non-value-adding activity, we must smooth the flow of people, materials, and information through all process steps.

To make the value stream flow, we match the rate of production to the rate of market consumption—no faster or slower—just in time to meet our customer's need. This supply chain management is complex but by no means impossible. To do so requires that we know three things very well.

First, we must know what our customer values so we can provide exactly what has been requested. Second, we must have an intimate understanding of our process characteristics, capabilities, and capacities. This helps us know what we should or, more importantly, what we should not do. Third, we must know our customer's timing. Our customer requires that our products be supplied at a particular rate. If we make them too slow the customer is deprived. If we make them too fast we create expensive and useless inventory. If we don't know our customer's timing, we can't match our rate of production to the rate of consumption and we'll be out of sequence.

To manage this timing issue, Lean uses something called *takt* time. *Takt* is a German word for an orchestra conductor's baton. Used in context, *takt* time means to keep time, to beat time, or to stay in time. The audience is the customer and the orchestra the provider. If the orchestra plays in time, the audience receives a satisfactory product. If the orchestra gets out of time, the audience receives a dissonant product—not what they paid for.

Takt time describes the rhythm of marketplace demand. We cannot match the rhythm of the marketplace if we don't know the *takt* time of the marketplace. This is critical because of seasonal buying fluctuations, fickle market conditions, or whatever is happening on Wall Street at the moment. Even a close approximation of what we should produce at any given time gives us a tremendous competitive edge, allowing us to do the right thing at the right time and better satisfy our customers.

Customer Pull

When we understand value, the value stream, and how to improve the flow of whatever it is we are producing, we can respond to customer pull. With Lean, the producer responds to the customer by replenishing what has been taken away— not by building inventory that may or may not be used at some point in the future. We strive to match our rate of replenishment to the timing of our customer's desire. The product must have a defined place to go—a vacuum, if you will. The product must fill an immediate need or we shouldn't make it. As we saw in 2008, making more automobiles than the market demands can cause real problems.

Producing what the customer wants, when the customer wants it, in the quantities the customer has asked for, is flow responding to pull. This is all done just in time to meet the customer's emerging needs and the *takt* of the marketplace. If we pull the product through the system in response to the customer's desire, rather than pushing it toward an unknown end, we neither create useless inventories nor consume valuable resources unnecessarily. By responding to pull, we flow the product to the customer at the customer's rate of consumption; we are Lean and have minimized our waste.

We can only pull the product through the process if we make small batches or one piece at a time, rather than large batches pushed toward an unknown end. By using Lean, our products move from one process to the next as soon as each value-adding step is completed. They do not wait in a stagnant inventory having already had value added to them but having no place to go because a large batch is occupying the next step. Processing large batches causes everything to wait because the first item in the batch cannot be used until the last item in the batch receives the same treatment.

Continuous Improvement

The engine that drives Lean Enterprise is a culture of continuous improvement that is clearly understood and supported by all members of the organization. Lean cannot be successfully implemented or managed without this consensual culture. Once we have established value-generating processes that flow smoothly in response to customer pull, we must have an ongoing mechanism to monitor the value stream to improve its performance and respond to changing market conditions. In a Lean environment, this involves all members of the organization regardless of rank or station. But it does not involve all members at the same time or in the same way. It involves each member according to that member's special knowledge, talents, and gifts. A separate chapter of this book has been reserved for how the leadership and followership work together to generate continuous improvement.

Key to implementing the five principles of Lean is using the special knowledge, talents, and gifts of each member of the organization. So different from what happens in many or most churches, Lean does not employ standing committees. Lean uses cross-functional teams of deliberately chosen individuals, each member being an expert in a particular subject area and each member representing other members of the larger organization like him or her. Each member of the team has a partial answer to nagging problems that just do not seem to go away. No single team member has the answer to a given problem. But, if the team members have been chosen properly, the whole team has the whole answer to any problem. The number of these teams, team membership, and the teams' missions change to address the needs of the value stream as those needs emerge. New teams are created and old teams are disbanded, as necessary, to address problems and implement improvements.

These are called *kaizen* teams. The Japanese word *kaizen* roughly translates as "small change for the better." *Kaizen* teams do not look for ways to comprehensively reengineer the entire process. They do not normally plan large capital expansions, nor do they do detailed market research or establish five-year strategic plans. They look for small ways to improve the operation—many small ways. They do not operate in a vacuum, but have specific guidelines and expectations. They do not strive to get the answer that someone already knows—they search for answers that people do not already know. *Kaizen* teams are not intended to replace the decision-making role of the organization's leadership. Their role is to support the leadership through study, analysis, and recommendation so the leadership can make better decisions. They use data, direct observation, and the knowledge and intuition of the people who are most intimately involved in doing the work and who experience the same problems day after day. *Kaizen's* purpose is to use the people who do the work to cut the waste out of the work. By doing so, *kaizen* becomes the enabler for the larger organization to dream larger dreams, fulfill deeper and wider visions, and accomplish more with the same or fewer resources.

ELEVATION CHURCH—Charlotte, NC
A Case Study

An example of Lean in a spiritual context is demonstrated by Elevation Church of Charlotte, NC. They own almost no, if any, facilities, which is a very Lean approach, giving them a unique approach to twenty-first-century ministry.

Moreover, by partnering with existing, effective, community nonprofits they provide an outstanding example of broad-spectrum *kaizen* in action in the church. By harnessing their efforts to already-established specialty disciplines in the community they achieve common strategic spiritual goals and focus their efforts outward rather than inward.

The following is reproduced from their website: www.elevationchurch.org/outreach:

Many churches have people who are passionate about feeding the hungry in their city, and they feel the need to start a food pantry—so they do. The youth group adopts a neighborhood, the seniors read to the kids at the school, the women's ministry serves food at Thanksgiving, the men start a remodeling ministry and on and on it goes. All of these things are wonderful but here is the problem: spreading out the leaders, resources and man-power will exert maximum effort while achieving minimal impact.

At Elevation we have decided to flip this model of church outreach on its head. Rather than spread everything out, we're focusing! We are concentrating all our efforts on several strategic community outreach partners that are already knocking it out of the park in our city! Currently, Elevation is partnered with twenty different organizations in the city of Charlotte. Our goal is to continue to reach out to our city through partnerships that are making a difference.

We are often asked, "How can a non-profit become a community outreach partner of Elevation?" Since we strive to develop strategic partnerships focused on community impact we are very strategic in our selection of community outreach partners. Key characteristics include sound resource stewardship and effective volunteer engagement processes, since we're committed to engaging our people in service with our partners. Each fiscal year, we review all of our partnerships regarding their effectiveness and their plans for the year ahead. If your organization is interested in submitting a grant proposal to Elevation, please view our application.

Dr. Don Pope
Professor of Management
Abilene Christian University

Chapter 3

The Necessity of Lean Ministry Today

"Weaving down the American highway
Through the litter and the wreckage and the cultural junk
Bloated with entitlement; loaded on propaganda
and now we're driving dazed and drunk."
"Long Road Out of Eden"
– The Eagles, 2007

As we said earlier, there is an impressive collection of contemporary work describing the condition of the twenty-first-century church, its problems, strengths, and what we should do to effectively and efficiently meet the needs of a changing world. This chapter is not intended to be a literature review. But, rather than repeat already excellent research in toto, we have selected four authors who we believe give a representative view of the landscape. We quote them freely in the following pages and augment their comments with our own. These authors and their relevant works are:

- Alan Hirsch, *The Forgotten Ways: Reactivating the Missional Church*
- David Kinnaman and Gabe Lyons, *unChristian: What a New Generation Really Thinks about Christianity . . . and Why It Matters*
- David T. Olson, *The American Church in Crisis: Groundbreaking Research Based on a National Database of over 200,000 Churches*
- Stanley J. Grenz, *A Primer on Postmodernism*.

What Is the Problem?

To respond to a problem one has to know what the problem is. This sounds simpler than it really is because often we identify only symptoms and not root causes. A problem can be seen either subjectively or objectively—but subjective analysis is of little value since everyone has an opinion and that opinion is always right. In contrast, rational decision-making dictates that we define the problem and its impact on our world using objective information. We must objectively understand the root causes to a problem before we can apply rational solutions. Defining a problem objectively requires facts. Our God is a factual God; our God is a rational God.

We believe the problem is this:

> We, the church, are failing to respond to a world in flux in a way that world finds acceptable. Our message is the same but we are using archaic methodologies to convey it, and we have developed behaviors resulting in problems of both form and function. The problem of form is that our behaviors alienate us from the world we are commissioned to reach. The problem of function is that we cannot develop or deploy an adequate response when our individual worlds continue to drift apart. Those of us who live in the insular world of the traditional church may think it's working but the facts say otherwise.

Stanley Grenz says that we are now moving into a new context. The Western world is turning from the Enlightenment principles that formed the foundation for modernity. We are entering the postmodern era. The shift from the familiar territory of modernity to the uncharted terrain of postmodernity has grave implications for those who seek to live as Christ's disciples in the new context. We must think through the ramifications of the phenomenal changes occurring in Western society to understand how we must present the gospel to the next generation.

How the Problem Came to Be a Problem

The following few paragraphs are paraphrased from Grenz's *A Primer on Postmodernism*. Evangelicalism shares close ties with modernity and, as modern thinkers, evangelicals have generally used the tools of modernity, such as the scientific method, the empirical approach to reality, and common sense realism. Twentieth- and now twenty-first-century evangelicals devoted much energy to demonstrating the credibility of the Christian faith to a culture that glorified reason and deified science. For a long time our culture has worshiped science as irrefutable—that has begun to change. Most of you reading this book are, like us, products of modernity—or at least you are well steeped in it. The world around us has changed subtly and slowly, but inexorably, to the point where we can scarcely recognize what we see out the window. Hirsch, Kinnaman, Olson, and Grenz clearly show that American culture has deteriorated into a fragmented series of neo-pagan and neo-tribal associations with conflicting value systems existing side-by-side.

Whatever it may become, postmodernism began as a rejection of the mind-set launched under the conditions of modernity. The abandonment of the belief in universal truth entails the loss of any final criterion by which to evaluate the various interpretations of reality that compete in the contemporary intellectual realm. In this situation, all human interpretations are equally valid or invalid. Postmodern skepticism leaves us in a world characterized by a never-ending struggle among competing interpretations. Our commitment to the God revealed in Christ compels us to stand squarely against at least one aspect of the radical skepticism of postmodernism—the loss of a center.

In contrast to postmodern thought, we believe there is a unifying center to reality. We acknowledge that this center has appeared in Jesus of Nazareth, who is the eternal Word present among us. We must not affirm the central tenet of postmodernism—the rejection of the Metanarrative. We firmly believe that the local narratives of the many human communities do fit together into a single grand narrative—the story of humankind. As Christians, we believe there is a single Metanarrative encompassing all peoples and all times. But postmodern thinkers rightly alert us to the naiveté of the Enlightenment attempt to discover universal truth by appealing to reason alone. In fact, the Metanarrative we proclaim lies beyond mere reason—for God is supernatural and will maintain a measure of mystery.

We cannot allow Christianity to be relegated to the status of one more faith among others. Christianity embodies *the* truth—the truth of, and for, all humankind. As Christians, we must stand against the postmodern rejection of the Metanarrative and not share in the despair over the loss of universality that leads to radical skepticism.

The problem became a problem for us by the church becoming distanced from the world around it. We didn't deliberately move away from the world. The world deliberately moved away from us. No matter; we are distanced because we have denied the reality of that change. Even though our message has remained the same—as it should—our lack of effectiveness is an indictment on our intractable behaviors. It is egocentric in the extreme to expect the world to overlook our inconsistencies when we refuse to overlook theirs.

The Renaissance followed the Dark Ages and precipitated social, political, intellectual, and cultural changes throughout the world starting in Europe and continuing between the fourteenth and seventeenth centuries. This gave way to the Enlightenment Period and the Age of Reason. The Enlightenment era in Western philosophy focused on intellectual, scientific, and cultural development in which reason was advocated as the primary source for legitimacy and the authority in all matters—principal among which was science and scientific method. Beginning somewhere in the eighteenth century (opinions differ), the Enlightenment Period gave way to modernity which took Enlightenment Period or Enlightenment Project thoughts, philosophies, and practices and focused them on the social conditions resulting from capitalism. The Enlightenment Period is generally considered to have ended about the year 1970. Following this came postmodernity, where we find ourselves today. Postmodernity is the air we breathe, whether we like it or not. If, as Stanley Grenz says, Friedrich Nietzsche initiated the postmodern ethos by announcing the death of God and proclaiming the advent of the Superhuman in 1883, this change has taken some time to mature—but it's here in force.

Other twentieth-century philosophers jumped to support Nietzsche's original thesis—preeminent among them were Michael Foucault, Jacques Derrida, and Michael Rorty. These three men were widely influential in systematically dismantling the culture of modernity. Their efforts were, in large part, responsible for our present-day culture's disillusionment and often outright rejection of Christendom. They reasoned that Christianity has been central to Christendom for 1700 years and Christendom central to modernity for the past 300–400 years. So it was their duty to dismantle Christianity as well.

Grenz claims postmodernism came of age in the U.S. with the death of Michael Foucault on June 25, 1948. Yet there were many other factors contributing to postmodernism hitting its stride in the U.S., not the least of which was how badly we handled the Vietnam War and the subsequent disillusionment with what was referred to in the late '60s and early '70s as "The Establishment."

What we call the church had been central to our accepted cultural norms since it was institutionalized as part of the state by Emperor Constantine's Edict of Milan in 313 AD and the First Council of Nicaea in 325 AD. Christendom has formed and reformed throughout the past 1700 years. Denominations and centers of influence have come and gone. But for the past 1700 years Christendom and Christianity have looked pretty much the same and have maintained certain defining characteristics. Some of them are:
- The local church has been the cultural center of the community.
- Each local church has drawn to it a people group of a rather homogenous ilk with few cultural or socioeconomic differences.
- The local church has been held up as representing moral authority and has been more or less accepted as such by those around it.

- The people group at hand has been expected to go to the church rather than the church go to them.
- If the local church did go to a people group apart from its cultural center it went to a people group of such unusual distinction and of such geographical separation as to fall into a separate category of ministry.
- The local church has been considered a birthing room for the development and refinement of art and music.
- Finally, irrespective of its official separation from the state, the church in the U.S. continues to be heavily involved in politics, just like it was for a time in Italy, Spain, France, and Great Britain.

That may have worked well for 1650 years or so but Hirsch, Grenz, Olson, and Kinnaman (among many others) say that it isn't working very well now. Over the past few decades we, as a culture, have rejected modernity and the Metanarrative. We have transitioned away from an agrarian-based culture having at its center the small town and the local church. We have largely rejected the concept of ultimate truth and the attendant behaviors it predicates. We have begun to see the church as something dangerous that threatens our individuality and freedom of choice.

Our postmodern, post-Christian culture bears little resemblance to that in which most of us were raised. To help clarify this contrast, postmodernism can be distilled into three characteristics:

First: Denial of an ultimate truth or standard against which all our beliefs, behaviors and actions are to be compared and judged as either right, wrong, true or untrue.

Second: Denial, or at best non-acceptance, of an overarching Metanarrative telling the story of humankind, where we came from—including the creation story—where we're going, and how God intends to take us there. The postmodern ethos does not accept the Metanarrative as spoken by God and therefore it is not the standard against which all sub-cultural narratives must be subordinated and compared for validity and truth.

Third: The postmodern ethos embraces heretofore conflicting systems of logic not only permitting but encouraging incompatible belief structures and standards of behavior to coexist side-by-side within cultural subgroups. These subgroups often have diametrically opposed beliefs, values, truths and untruths, and rights and wrongs—but each subgroup is considered to be equally valid.

We are no longer a mono-ethnic, semi-literate, marginally healthy, and immobile agrarian and manufacturing culture that corporately embraces a commonly understood set of morals and values rooted in a standard not of our own manufacture. We are now a multi-ethnic, highly-educated, healthy, service- and technology-oriented, metro-suburban culture that is moving fluidly across the globe in small groups of neo-tribal cultures—each of which has embraced its own definitions of truth and right.

Postmodernity is comprised mostly of younger people who are rightly the future face of the Bride of Christ. Postmodernity causes our Christian young people to think differently and behave differently. If you doubt that, ask your teenagers for their opinion on the three points listed above. Their answers may shock you.

Those in positions of authority or those of us having occupied a particular pew for a generation or two may think we are directing the development of the Bride of Christ—but perhaps we are doing so less than we think. The real driving force in the church today is our Christian children who are setting expectations for change. They still want the same basic transformation that we want but they want it delivered differently. They want truth, even as all of us do, and they know best how to approach and deliver the message of Christ to their outsider friends. Their expectations create a vacuum that pulls the church toward them even as Christ pulls the individual toward Himself.

How Does the Problem Affect Us?

How the problem affects us might best be introduced through a personal experience. For me, Charles, this book culminates a twelve-year odyssey beginning with a corporate relocation to the Deep South in 1998. I like to tell the following story.

The most recent phase of my Christian life began in 1998 with a corporate relocation to a small city in north Alabama. We left a healthy and dynamic church in the town where we had lived in Wisconsin but were hopeful of finding a similar church in the middle of the Bible Belt. When we got there, the Yellow Pages showed a count of sixty-five evangelical churches in a town of 67,000 people. Our family of five was in high spiritual spirits and expectant of great things in the hunt for a new church. We figured we shouldn't have any trouble finding something to suit our needs with that many to pick from.

Nothing could have been further from the truth. We visited a number of churches only to find them austere and distant. The music was stiff and lacked passion. The sermons most often were salvation sermons being preached to a congregation full of people having been converted as children. Though the summer temperatures were approaching the 100s, the dress was formal—the men in suits and the women dressed to the nines. I, dressed in shorts and a Hawaiian shirt, could have been on my way to a Jimmy Buffet concert. It was frustrating, and after a few Sundays we took to discussing what we had either learned or not learned (mostly what we had not learned) over Sunday lunch at a local restaurant.

We finally settled on a well-established church from a mainline denomination in the center of town, having been a bulwark in the community since shortly after the Civil War, and we attended for a number of Sundays. It left us cold, but it was the best haven we could come up with. But why wasn't it working for us? It was a model of the churches I had attended as a child. All the elements were in place. It was a beautiful pre-War edifice. It was led by a dedicated staff of professional clergy. They used traditional music accompanied by a 200-pipe organ. The sanctuary was ornate and bespoke majesty and was filled with well-dressed and dignified people, each with a firm and respectful handshake.

Nothing was wrong per se; in fact, it was very right by the standards my wife and I had grown up with. But still, it wasn't working for us.

One Sunday, on our way to lunch after another less-than-inspiring worship experience, my fifteen-year-old daughter, Lauren, drew a line in the sand. To know her is to love her and to love her is to appreciate her somewhat macabre sense of humor—she's a funny gal.

On this particular Sunday, during a lull in the conversation on the way to lunch, she piped up saying, "I need to take a position on this church thing—just so everyone knows where I'm at on this subject."

There was silence in the car. She went on to say, "You know those little pencils in the back of the pews?"

We did. "Well," she said, "if you take me back to that church next Sunday I'm going to take one of those little pencils out of the pew in front of me and I'm going to gouge out my eyes. Then you'll have to lead me around by the hand for the rest of my life and everyone who sees me will know what you did to me. No pressure—I just want you to know."

Needless to say, I knew we had a problem. Three more corporate relocations followed over the next ten years, each accompanied by a difficult and frustrating search for a church home. This resulted in a long, dry period of not finding a comfortable church family of which to become a part.

The world, represented by the attitudes of my Christian children, had changed around me and I hadn't noticed.

We never went back to that particular church, and Lauren still has both eyes.

This story, although humorous, sadly defines a serious problem and its impact on our young people. It points to a monumental shift taking place before our very eyes. The shift is occurring both inside the church between Christians; and between the church and non-Christians outside the church. This gap must be bridged to make the church effective in its role as God's chosen tool to reach lives and be the organ of transformation when those lost lives are reached.

Of the books on the market today giving descriptions of the health of the twenty-first-century church, two stand in a class by themselves as having used purely objective methodologies to draw their conclusions. One is *unChristian* by David Kinnaman and Gabe Lyons of the Barna Group. The other is *The American Church in Crisis* by David Olson. They are seminal works and both draw conclusions from hard data gathered from real people who are living real lives.

You should know that we have high standards for data-based conclusions. This results from having been intimately associated with some rather sophisticated statistical methods in our careers. After reading both books, our conclusion is that the data-gathering and data-reduction methods used by these authors are sound. They conclude that the problem is real and has a real impact on real people in the U.S. and that Charles's earlier story is not an isolated example. Both say church health is failing in the U.S. and give hard data to support their findings.

The Problem of Form

David Kinnaman is president of The Barna Group, the Christian data-gathering organization that provides research and resources to facilitate spiritual transformation in people's lives. His coauthor, Gabe Lyons, founded The Fermi Project, a broad collective of innovators, social entrepreneurs, and church and societal leaders working together to make positive contributions to our culture. They describe our problem of form in detail in their book, *unChristian*, and say that the Christian community has gone from a position of esteem to a position of disdain in ten short years for six specific reasons. We are seen as being:

1. Hypocritical
2. Too focused on getting converts
3. Anti-homosexual
4. Sheltered
5. Too political
6. Judgmental

The main group studied in the book is what they are calling *outsiders*—those looking at the Christian faith from the outside. This group includes atheists, agnostics, those affiliated with a faith other than Christianity such as Islam, Hinduism, Judaism, Mormonism, etc., and other unchurched adults who are not born-again Christians.

Two terms describe the primary generations studied:
- Mosaics (born between 1984 and 2002)
- Busters (born between 1965 and 1983).

Even though many of these people are "outsiders" they are potentially the future Bride of Christ. To say the following findings are shocking is the understatement of the ages.

Fewer than one out of ten young adults mention faith as their top priority, despite the fact that the majority of Busters and Mosaics attended a Christian church during their high school years.

In 1996, 85% of outsiders were favorable toward Christianity's role in society. Now, 38% claim to have a bad impression of present-day Christianity. One-third of young outsiders said that Christianity represents a negative image with which they would not want to be associated. Seventeen percent of young outsiders indicate that they maintain very bad perceptions of the Christian faith. In fact, negative opinions of Christians outnumbered positive perceptions 35% to 10%. Their views on the term *evangelical* were extraordinarily negative at 49% as opposed to 3% positive.

The three most common perceptions of present-day Christianity held by young outsiders are: anti-homosexual (91%), judgmental (87%), and hypocritical (85%). Of the top twelve perceptions of Christianity, nine were negative. The most common favorable impression, if it could be considered favorable, is that Christianity teaches the same basic idea as other religions—more than 80% of young outsiders embrace this flawed perception. Three-quarters believe that Christianity has good values and principles, and most outsiders indicate that Christians are friendly.

Consider the following astonishing fact. The vast majority of the outsiders Kinnaman surveyed within the Mosaic and Buster generations have been to churches before; most have attended at least one church for several months; nearly nine out of ten say they know Christians personally; in fact, each has about five friends who are believers.

Young outsiders' views of Christianity are forged through a wide range of inputs: experiences at churches (59%) and relationships (50%) are the most common. This is followed by input from other religions (48%) and what their parents have told them about Christianity (40%). Only 9% of young outsiders and only 22% of young churchgoers said that Christianity has received a bad reputation from television and movies.

One-fifth of all outsiders, regardless of age, admitted they have had a bad experience in a church or with a Christian that gave them a negative image of Jesus Christ. This represents nearly 50 million adult residents of this country—including about 9 million young outsiders—who admit they have significant emotional or spiritual baggage from past experiences with so-called Christ followers.

Three out of ten young outsiders said they have undergone negative experiences in churches and with Christians. Such hurtful experiences are part of the stories of nearly one out of every two young people who are atheists, agnostics, or of some other faith. Outsiders who are Mosaics and Busters are 2.5 times more likely than older outsiders to say bad experiences have degraded their picture of Jesus.

Many young Christians harbor significant concerns about the Christian faith as well. For instance, four out of five young churchgoers say that Christianity is anti-homosexual; half describe it as judgmental, too involved in politics, hypocritical, and confusing; one-third believe their faith is old fashioned and out of touch with reality; one-quarter of young Christians believe Christianity is boring and insensitive to others.

Here's another heartbreaking fact: a majority of young Christians said that when deciding how to spend their time, they try to choose activities that will help bring people closer to Christ. Most indicate that they intentionally build friendships with other people so they might get a chance to explain their faith in Jesus. And, yet, they are put in a position of constant self-defense.

The problem is real.

The Problem of Function

David Olson is the Director of Church Planting for the Evangelical Covenant Church, a rapidly growing multi-ethnic denomination, who, as a hobby, has been collecting research data on church health for the last fifteen years. This research grew out of his frustration that no one really knew how the American church was doing and Christian leaders were often making wild guesses and declarative statements based on inaccurate hearsay. Exaggerating the challenges, overestimating the progress, or ignoring reality have been common Christian responses to the missional challenges for Christians in the United States. This research was undertaken because we cannot know where to go and how to get there until we find out where we are and why we are in that situation. David Olson's findings culminated in his recent book *The American Church in Crisis.*

The question, "How healthy is the twenty-first-century church?" is not a simple one. Olson's summary answer to that question is the lead-off statement on page 15 of the introduction where he affirms that the book was aptly titled.

To collect and reduce his data into meaningful conclusions, Olson uses the Lean approach called the *Plan-Do-Check-Act Cycle.* His reference for doing so is the book of Numbers which employs a similar four-stage process for assessing our spiritual health. He uses slightly different words, but the concept is the same.

He calls his steps:
1. Observation
2. Evaluation
3. Introspection
4. Action

Olson looks at four types of churchgoers over three categories of churches. The church categories he looked at are: evangelical, mainline, and Catholic. The four types of churchgoers surveyed are:
- Weekly attendees: The average population of Americans attending a Christian worship service on a given week.
- Regular attendees: Someone who attends a Christian church on a consistent basis; i.e., at least three out of every eight Sundays.
- Active members: Those who attend a Christian church once per month or less and occasionally give some money to the church.
- Inclusive members: People who report belonging to a particular church tradition but have no authentic connection as demonstrated by their actions.

Any analysis is subject to error but his liability is compounded by the fact that people generally do not tell the truth about their churchgoing behaviors and report a more devoted behavior than actually exists. To compensate, he uses statistical modeling to minimize these errors and fine-tune the following conclusions.

- A reasonable estimate is that 17.4% of Americans attend a Christian church on any given Sunday, broken down by:
  - o Evangelical: 9.1%
  - o Mainline: 3%
  - o Catholic: 5.3%
- An additional 5.5% are regular attendees, for a running total of 23%.
- Another 14% are active members who attend church and occasionally contribute some money, for a running total of 37%.
- Finally, an additional 15% claim affiliation but has no real connection, for a total of 52%.
- Conclusion: Fifty-two percent of Americans consider themselves inclusive members, but only 23% demonstrate their faith through active participation in a church.

Central to Olson's research are the questions of whether the twenty-first-century church is at least keeping up with population growth in this country and what that finding means for the church's future. He gives detailed findings of evangelical, mainline, and Catholic churches by state and county, including church closings, church starts, and detailed discussions of why churches thrive or decline.

He adjusts his findings to account for population growth through births, deaths, and immigration. Then he extrapolates where we should expect to be in the coming years against where we actually are today. He discusses denominational winners and losers and the reasons for whatever is happening to each. He talks about why it is critical to plant churches and how much easier it is to plant a new church than to revive an old one.

For our purposes we go directly to the big-picture questions of: Are we keeping up with population growth, and what does this look like for the future? The answers are discouraging. Attendance in a Christian church is not keeping up with population growth, and if present trends continue, it will fall even further behind in the near future.

Olson found that:
- 17% of established churches are stable;
- 31% of established churches are growing;
- 52% of established churches are declining.

He takes it to the next level and finds that between the years 1990 and 2010:
- Total church attendance declined from 20.4% to 16.5%.
  - o It will continue to decline to 14.5% by the year 2020
- Evangelical church attendance declined from 9.2% to 8.9%.
  - o It will continue to decline to 8.5% by the year 2020
- Mainline church attendance declined from 3.9% to 2.7%.
  - o It will continue to decline to 2.1% in 2020.
- Catholic church attendance declined from 7.1% to 4.8%.
  - o It will continue to decline to 4.0% in 2020.
- Between the years 1990 and 2005 church attendance in the U.S. did not keep up with population growth in any state.

Unless there is a substantive change in the Christian community in both form and function, the established church will continue to atrophy.

A summary of recommendations by the aforementioned four authors follows.

David Kinnaman and Gabe Lyons

Kinnaman and Lyons say that if we wish to change how we are perceived in the world we need to change how we relate to the people we need to reach. We must really know people, not just know *about* them. We must address their needs as well as their criticisms through our service to and our sacrifice for them. We must do four things.

1. Respond with the right perspective. We must adopt Jesus' right perspective and not be defined by our enemies. Jesus looked below the surface at people's true motives to address their core spiritual needs. The Bible says we will not be popular and the gospel will not make sense to outsiders (1 Corinthians 1–3). But, if we respond to criticism with anger and defensiveness, we simply validate their indictment of us. Jesus never responded with anger to His unchurched critics— He looked deeper to see what was really driving the behavior. Our response to cynicism must be motivated by our desire to glorify God, not to defend our own tarnished behaviors.

2. Connect with people. Jesus related to His disciples through friendships. This forged bonds so strong they were willing to give up everything and follow Him, endure privation and hardship, and even die for Him. Humankind is most often influenced through the intimacy of personal relationships. The Kinnaman and Lyons research found that the negative perceptions of outsiders can be overcome through meaningful and trusting relationships with Christians who live the gospel instead of simply talk about it. Consider the impact of 20 million Christians on our culture if each were to engage only one outsider in a meaningful, loving, non-judgmental, and genuine Christlike relationship.

3. Be creative. The Mosaics and the Busters represent the future of the church, and they are hungry for meaning in their lives, including creative yet non-compromising expressions of the good news of the gospel. Our young people speak a different language. What was meaningful and even profound to us has become trite to them. Their needs are the same as ours—redemption, impact, and intimacy—but we cannot simply quote Scripture to a generation who has little knowledge of the Bible. We must be creative enough to simplify it and put it into a context with meaning for their lives. We take for granted that we are all singing off the same page. In fact, we are no longer on the same page with the future leaders of the church—we are not even in the same hymnal. We must make the effort to creatively communicate Jesus' message to a generation that harbors deep cynicism toward Christianity. We must be simple. We must be clear. Our biggest challenge is how to communicate the authority of the Bible, and the eternal impact of the gospel, to a generation that no longer accepts the Metanarrative and is impervious to our claim that the Bible represents truth.

4. Serve people. Many outsiders say Christians are poor listeners. This is a major indictment because it reeks of arrogance. We must cultivate genuine deep concern and sensitivity to the needs of outsiders, and that begins with listening. We cannot fake it. We either truly care or we don't; outsiders can tell the difference. True care is manifested in tangible service. We must regain our heart for outsiders and we cannot wait until they are spiritually groomed and coiffed to meet our standards. Jesus ministered to prostitutes and sinners (Mark 2:16-7). If we ask Him, God will graciously provide us opportunities to serve as well.

David Olson

David Olson estimates that a successful reversal of the present trends in the church will take fifteen to twenty years and that it is five to seven times easier to plant a new church than it is to revitalize an established church. But he does see it as reversible and an opportunity to restore Jesus' words and actions to their place of centrality in the twenty-first-century church. He suggests a ten-step approach for the American church to have a bright future.

1. Those in leadership positions must be honest about what is happening in the American church, and in their denominations, and personally lead the church forward in spirituality, chemistry, and strategy.

2. Established churches, and all their membership, must have the courage and commitment to focus on and deliberately pursue health and growth.
3. Leadership must accept that we live in, and must learn to thrive in, a post-Christian, postmodern, and multiethnic world.
4. The most effective attitude, model, and mission strategy will be that of the early church to the Greco-Roman world.
5. Pastors must upgrade their ministry gifts and skills to articulate our mission with passion, power, and wisdom.
6. All Christians must engage their neighbors with a humble and listening attitude and relish these new opportunities as gifts from God.
7. Established churches must embrace church planting as the primary method of passing the faith to future generations.
8. Denominations must develop mammalian church-planting structures while simultaneously encouraging church planting to develop at the grassroots level.
9. Leadership must devote more time to raising up and training young leaders in churches, colleges, and community organizations.
10. The church must recognize anew the importance of the Holy Spirit in the life of the church.

Alan Hirsch

In *The Forgotten Ways*, Alan Hirsch mounts a convincing and compelling argument for success by saying that we must rediscover something he calls "Apostolic Genius." He believes the following six elements of Apostolic Genius can get us back on the right track.

1. Jesus is Lord. Our faith and everything that it hopes to accomplish must be Christocentric—the epicenter of Apostolic Genius being Jesus as Lord. Our submission to Jesus as Lord over everything that was, that is, and that will be is a simple statement but a confession that vibrates with the primal energies of scriptural faith. We must fully accept that there is one God over every aspect of every life, and submission to the one true God must predicate everything that we do.

2. Disciple-making. This is the irreplaceable and lifelong task of becoming like Jesus by embodying His message. Disciple-making, or what we are calling the transformation process, is the core task of the church and needs to be structured into every church's basic formula.

3. Missional-Incarnational impulse.   There must be twin impulses to any remarkable missional movement. Namely, the dynamic outward thrust and the related deepening impulse, which together seed and embed the gospel in different cultures and people groups. We must be Jesus Christ incarnate to the world outside the walls of the church.

4. Apostolic environment.   Our leadership must deliberately foster a fertile environment of apostolic influence to initiate and maintain phenomenal movements of God and to sustain metabolic growth and impact on what we are asked to do.

5. Organic systems.   We must have appropriate structures for healthy metabolic growth. These structures must be flexible, fluid, and unconstrained by central controls which block growth. Further, these structures must apply to the people group at hand and they must be structures embodying a minimum of waste.

6. Communitas, not community.   The most vigorous forms of community are those that come together in the context of a shared ordeal or those that define themselves as a group with a mission that lies beyond them. Healthy communitas will not overemphasize safety and security, nor focus on comfort and convenience, but on our true calling and purpose.

Stanley Grenz

Stanley Grenz sees Christians as having more in common with the postmodern generation than at first glance. You can decide yourself how close to the boundary of postmodern thought you wish to live; that is beyond the scope of this book. Yet, Dr. Grenz has insight to offer those of us who are decidedly not postmodern. He says that much of the present ethos can work to our advantage if we are willing to see the big picture and respond as we should have been responding for some time. Evangelicals have often uncritically accepted the modern view of knowledge despite the fact that, at certain points, the postmodern critique is more in keeping with Christian theological understandings. One commonality is that Christianity denies that the rational, scientific method is the sole measure of truth. Truth is embodied in what we do not know about God—His mystery—as well as what we do know about God. He has four recommendations for how we can better communicate the gospel to a postmodern world.

1. Post-individualistic gospel.   One of the hallmarks of modernity is the elevation of the individual. We must always keep in mind the biblical themes of God's concern for each person, the accountability of every human being before God, and the individual orientation that lies within the salvation message. But we must shake ourselves loose from the modern mind-set of radical individualism. Like postmoderns we must affirm that knowledge—including knowledge of God—is not only objective. Knowledge of God is primarily objectively discovered, but not solely so. Objective truth must be the guide and prism through which all subjective discoveries are evaluated. Knowledge of God is secondarily discovered through communities, and communities are more important to postmodernity than they were to modernity. God is the perfect social Trinity—Father, Son, and Spirit—indicating that the divine purpose for creation is directed toward the individual-in-relationship.

2. Post-rationalistic gospel. The second hallmark of modernity is the elevation of reason. Modern evangelicals have painstakingly attempted to demonstrate that the Christian faith is not unreasonable. We proclaim that one must not commit intellectual suicide in order to be a Christian. Postmoderns should not become anti-intellectual, but should also acknowledge that intellect and science alone cannot put us in touch with every dimension of reality or lead us to discover every aspect of God's truth. We must make room for the concept of mystery— as a reminder that God's reality transcends human reason. At the heart of our Christian experience is the mystery of a personal encounter with God in Christ.

3. Post-dualistic gospel. The Enlightenment divided reality into two categories: mind and matter. This dualism affected the view of the human person as soul, or thinking substance, and body, or physical substance. This has strongly influenced evangelical thinking. Modern evangelicals often articulate a dualistic gospel with the primary, if not sole, concern being the salvation of souls. They may entertain a secondary concern for bodies, but behave as if the physical dimension has no eternal importance. The next generation is interested in the human person as a unified whole. The gospel we proclaim must speak to human beings in their entirety, including the tangible and intangible aspects of the individual. Our Lord spoke about, and ministered to, people as whole persons and performed miracles touching their souls as well as healing their bodies. He responded to them as persons-in-relationship to their whole world.

4. Post-noeticentric Gospel. The gospel must affirm that the goal of our existence encompasses more than just the accumulation of knowledge. The purpose of correct doctrine is the attainment of wisdom and obedience, and the ultimate glorification of God. We should not be under the illusion that knowledge, even biblical knowledge, is inherently good, unless it results in some positive change – as Paul demonstrates in 1 Corinthians 8:1. Commitment to Christ cannot remain intellectual but must take lodging in the heart. Postmoderns are correct to remind us that we will be able to sustain right action only when it flows from the resources of the Holy Spirit, who continually renews our inner person.

Our Synthesis

We offer the following synthesis, in addition to our comments on the previous pages, to augment these four authors' arguments. These books were written by men with different backgrounds using different approaches. But with only minor differences, they all sing the same song: the twenty-first-century church has a problem, and the Plaintiffs have some very good points. We brought the problem on ourselves, and if we don't do something about it, the church as we know it will continue to decline and much of it will perish. But whatever changes we make, we must preserve the integrity of what God has spoken through His revealed Word (2 Timothy 3:16–17), as well as embrace the essential composition and needs of the believer as sacrosanct. It is the behavior of the church that must change (1 Corinthians 9:21–23).

The church must go to the people it hopes to reach rather than expect them to come to us—demonstrated by the use of the word "Go" in Jesus' Great Commission (Matthew 28:18–20). Our leadership must deliberately develop and nurture sustainable reproductive systems. The flexibility of the local church must not be hampered by central controls. The church must see both insiders and outsiders as persons-in-relationship—all of whom are searching for the intimacy represented by the gospel.

Is this really a problem or is it an opportunity? Does it have to be one or the other—or could it be both at the same time. It is trite to say that one man's problem is another man's opportunity—but also true. To properly respond, we must appraise where we find ourselves. We cannot do an honest appraisal if we are hunkered down pretending that the problem doesn't exist or hoping that it will go away.

The U.S. Marine Corps School of Infantry doctrine deals with, among other things, the subject of ambush. Ambush is a fact of life, be it in a military or non-military context. USMC infantry doctrine says that you have enemies and your enemies wish to harm or kill you. You will be ambushed. It is not a potentiality—it is an eventuality. If you do not take quick and decisive action when you are ambushed, you will die. In an ambush situation you have three choices. First, you can stand your ground. Second, you can retreat. Third, you can turn and rush into the enemy. Two of these choices are wrong—one is right. Standing your ground is a wrong choice because it maintains your position in the enemy's kill zone. By standing your ground you validate your role as target. They have chosen the terrain because it gives them the advantage. They have chosen the timing because it augments their advantage. If you stay in their kill zone they will kill you no matter how much you may wish to live or how hard you fight. Retreating is another wrong choice. If you retreat you remove yourself from the kill zone but you actually do something worse than standing your ground. You give the enemy a further advantage beyond terrain and timing—you show them your back. They will chase you and kill you. The third option, as frightening as it is, is the only one that is correct. It is one from which anyone with even the slightest self-preservation instinct will recoil. But it is the best option for saving your life—you must turn and rush into the enemy. Doing so does several things. First, it brings them into their own kill zone. Second, it puts you on their turf—a position of equality. Third, it meets force with force—not what they were expecting. As frightening as this might be, it is your only hope of survival. You must turn and rush into the enemy.

The twenty-first-century church has been ambushed. We are in peril. Our enemy has us on his terrain and has brilliantly timed his assault. The hard data says we are taking casualties. We are falling and we have no choice but to turn and rush into the enemy—bringing him into his own kill zone, occupying the same terrain as he, and meeting his force with an even more terrible force.

It is unfortunate that the twenty-first-century church often doesn't know who the enemy is. We behave as if outsiders are the enemy instead of seeing outsiders as precisely whom God has sent us to rescue (Romans 10:1–17). Likewise, we often also see those inside the church as our enemies because of slight, peripheral differences. Often we eat our own young in the church by stifling their creative spiritual energies when our young should be seen as our greatest resource and the future of the church.

Outsiders are not the enemy. We inside the church are not the enemy. But we inside the church can become our own worst enemy if we allow ourselves to buy into that deception. Our young are not the enemy; they are our greatest resource and always will be. Our enemy is Satan—and Satan is bent on our destruction (1 Peter 5:8). It is him whom we fight.

To fight and win we need to change both our strategy and our tactics. Change begins with a realistic appraisal of who we are, and what we are supposed to accomplish. To get realistic answers to these questions we need to brutally assess our weaknesses. We need to be naked before God.

This is not just a problem—it is an opportunity.

Lean methodology can help us see God as He really is, and to know His desires as He knows them. Seeing Him as He really is and knowing His desires as He knows them will help us see ourselves as we really are and how we should respond to Him. To make this change in focus and behavior we need a proven methodology with simplicity, flexibility, and speed. It must characterize the problem as it exists in our local churches and frankly assess strengths and weaknesses. We need a process that will transform criticism provided by outsiders into improvements inside our ministries. We need a process that will allow us to compromise our historical biases in favor of what's right. We must refocus our energies on the realities of our Christian experience—not our perceptions. We can recreate the wheel in each situation and each venue or we can use something that already works.

We must lead at two levels. We must see the big picture and lead strategically. But we must also acknowledge that the big picture is composed of the tactics of many individual personal encounters. We must own the fact that each individual transformation is initiated through a face-to-face encounter between people, just as each of us individually encounters Jesus. The starting point for successful transformation was, is now, and will forever be, through individual loving relationships and service to individuals. We must see ourselves and others as persons-in-relationship. We must minister one person at a time, just as Jesus transforms people one life at a time. We must have the courage to eliminate elements of our historical and cultural experience that no longer serve a constructive purpose. We must shed this waste. Lean ministry can provide the template to accomplish that task.

LIFEBRIDGE CHURCH—Madison, MS
Using Flow and Pull to Facilitate Transformation

LifeBridge is a church plant in Madison, Mississippi that has reached a sustainable level. It has not had any outside funding for several years, has slowly grown its staff to three full-time professionals, and hopes to begin construction on its first building this year. Founding Pastors Philip Thurman and Greg Miller started LifeBridge five years ago as an externally-focused church that targets unchurched people, specifically, the thirty-five-year-old married male.

Because LifeBridge has been successful at reaching its target, one of its biggest needs is to help new believers and people returning to church after many years to engage in a spiritual growth process.

LifeBridge views an individual's spiritual growth as a key transformation process. The staff has spent significant time considering how that typically could work and has done several things to understand and encourage a God-ordained flow for this process. One key part of the flow of this process is encouraging people to read the Bible daily and apply it to their lives. Philip, Greg, and the rest of the staff are convinced that the pull of the Holy Spirit is most powerful when people are reading and thinking about the truths in God's Word.

An example of how LifeBridge encourages the proper flow is its offering of daily devotionals. This process has developed over the past year from simply listing suggested readings, to a volunteer effort that produces weekly-specific verses and application questions related to the previous Sunday's message. Tying devotionals to the most recent Sunday's teaching is designed to make it easier for people to connect what they hear on Sunday with how they live their lives. These verses and questions are listed on the back of the bulletin and are also sent via a mass e-mail each day.

E-mail is considered one of the more effective ways to encourage daily reading. The e-mails (also readable on smart phones) are sent at 2 a.m. each day and include the verses and questions on one page. Many attendees tell the staff that this e-mail is the first thing they read when they get to work. LifeBridge currently sends these daily e-mails to over 120 people, a significant portion of their typical Sunday adult worship service attendance of about 160.

An additional benefit of this use of flow is the leadership development opportunity for existing and potential volunteer leaders. This process gives the staff the opportunity to understand the abilities and spiritual maturity of the people who prepare these devotionals which they do in a rotational approach that gives each person several opportunities a year to prepare a week's worth of material based on the established preaching schedule.

It is still too early to know the full impact of this process flow, but LifeBridge is confident that it will continue to be an effective tool that the Holy Spirit will use to pull people toward spiritual growth.

– Johnny Ervin, LifeBridge Church

Chapter 4

A Bridge to Somewhere

"I'll take your part
When darkness comes
And pain is all around
Like a bridge over troubled water
I will lay me down."

– Paul Simon, 1969
"Bridge Over Troubled Water"

We, who are the Bride of Christ, are at once the process, processors, and product of the Christian transformation. We are all a part of God's system. Because God's system is stewarded by fallible human beings, it has both value-adding and non-value-adding activities. As leaders, it is our job to understand the difference and respond accordingly.

A lot has been written in the past ten years on the church adapting to meet the needs of a changing world, the operative word being "relevance." Many books on this subject are excellent, but most of them deal with specific situations and specific successes or failures. Then they attempt to extrapolate these situations to the church-at-large. Taken in total, this body of knowledge assesses a global set of problems facing the church today. When reading these books with an eye to establishing commonality between diverse examples, it is impossible to conclude anything other than this: successful churches employ Lean principles— even if they don't use that terminology—and unsuccessful churches most often do not.

Many contemporary authors (Alan Hirsch, David Kinnaman, David Olson, Thom Rainer, Eric Geiger, Tom Nebel, Gary Rohrmayer, Neil Cole, Christian Schwarz,

Stanley Grenz, and others) have pointed out rather bluntly that we have a problem. Many, if not most, churches use a ministry model that works less effectively each day. We cling to a central edifice, are governed by an elect few, focus on a one-way transfer of knowledge to shrinking congregations—all the while hoping the community around us will see the wisdom of darkening the doorstep of our church. In the meantime, the culture around us continues to fragment itself into a series of neo-tribal and often neo-pagan factions, each of which has its own value system and definition of truth. These value systems often conflict with each other, as well as with Christianity, widening the gaps between them and us. Too often the church is not seen as relevant because we, the church, have not adapted at the same rate that the world around us has changed.

To be sure, some churches have adapted to the postmodern culture, but they are on the fringes of our spiritual community. Other churches have changed and made themselves very accommodating for those seeking meaning in their lives. But some of these have either flatly compromised God's nature (Revelation 4:8) or the truth of what He has spoken through Jesus Christ (John 1) and His Word (2 Timothy 3:16-17). Too many mainline denominations, and not a few evangelical churches, are trudging along, burdened with a heavy load of waste, indulging in activities and programs the world sees as useless. Such programs only prevent us from effectively reaching out to a world in need (Matthew 28:18-20).

We must change and we must change quickly (1 Corinthians 9:24-27). Making ministry Lean will facilitate that change and bring us abreast of a culture that sees us as less meaningful each day. By determining the baseline reason for our existence—our Lord's values—we can refocus our efforts on what really matters.

Counting the Cost

Before going on, we need to say a few words about cost-cutting because it is a subject of significant focus in many churches. God cares more about how we use our wealth than about supporting business as usual. He only cares about wealth insomuch as it fits into His plan for humanity and for the transformation of the individual disciple.

He has a much grander plan in mind, involving eternal values that transcend televisions, automobiles, and houses bigger than we can use. If taken seriously, Jesus' admonition to us to "lose our life for His sake so that we may gain it," (Luke 9:24) tells us there is something profound afoot.

So, it is important to state that Lean is only indirectly about cutting your costs. Lean is about using what you have to accomplish more than you are now. Cost reduction is an indirect benefit—but it always occurs. This should be at least incidentally helpful for every Christian organization with which we are familiar.

Anyone can go out onto the factory floor or to the church office and say, "Okay, everybody stop what you're doing and go home now. We'll call you if we need you again." Cutting costs isn't hard, all you have to be able to do is count. So, if cutting costs is your focus, simply send some people home and quit paying them. Cut some programs and ministries as well. Doing so will indeed save money—but at what real cost? You might pay dearly for saving that money and becoming ineffective for God's purposes. And how do you know you did the right thing? You don't, unless you have some guidelines.

Lean cuts waste, and cutting waste is entirely different than simply cutting costs because to cut waste you first have to define waste relative to value. To do that, you need to understand value as defined by the customer. Cutting waste allows you to redeploy your resources to concentrate on what is really important to your customer. This is a key responsibility of church leadership. Our leaders must focus on the overall processes, not just walk around looking for ways to cut cost.

Two very significant things happen when you refocus your resources on what is important. The quality of your product improves, and the cost of your product is reduced. You can't miss, because cost reduction is a natural by-product of cutting waste. Sometimes cost reduction occurs at such a magnitude that many people refuse to believe it.

But, as Christians, cost cutting is only a small part of our mission. Our real mission is to glorify God (Romans 11:36).

Lean Ministry

The graphic presented in Chapter 2 has been expanded in Figure 4.1 on the next page to show how the five principles of Lean apply to ministry. There's a reason why the arrow goes only one way—it's a one-way street, each principle leading to the next. We start with an understanding of what our Lord values and proceed to each sequential step.

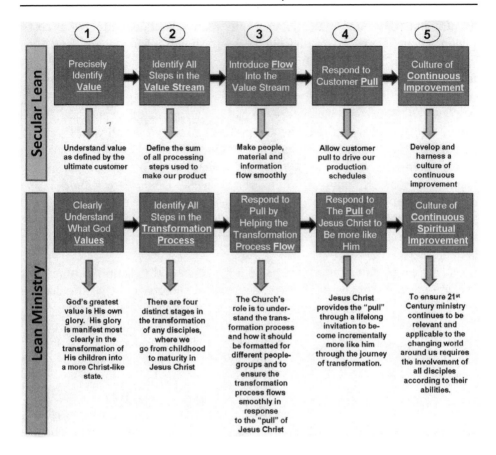

Figure 4.1: Lean Ministry

Anyone or anything exists to serve the needs or desires of someone or something else. From our human perspective, we reason that we take some positive action in order to gain something. To accomplish this gain more effectively, we form ourselves into organizations with both internal and external customers. Then we try to coordinate everything, our internal and external customers, our raw materials, and our processes, to achieve some gain for ourselves. Sometimes we do it well and sometimes not.

Yet we strive on because the human spirit is practical and our lives of toil are filled with what we hope are actions designed to generate improvement. With or without Lean, it is inconceivable to the productive human spirit not to take some action toward achieving something better. Every action we take is instrumental in nature—each action leads to something better which again leads to something better, and so on.

So, if every action attempts to achieve something good, which in turn leads to something even better, there must be some point that represents the highest good or the sum of all good things.

Aristotle took a run at this by attempting to define the highest good as that which has the following three characteristics:
- It is desirable for itself.
- It is not desirable for the sake of some other good.
- All other goods are desirable for its sake.

Unfortunately, Aristotle fell short by concluding that the highest good was to *live well*. We who are believers in Christ also have a need for systematic improvement, but that improvement must represent something more noble, and for a greater purpose, than *living well*.

Not the Voice of the Customer, but the Voice of Our Lord

To implement Lean in ministry we must first understand who our customer is. We began this book by looking at the needs of the church's internal customers—the individual disciples undergoing transformation. But it quickly became evident that if we didn't start at the beginning, with God Himself, we could construct a very lean ministry and efficiently do all the wrong things. So we went back to the source of our existence and began with God as a *customer* because any organization using Lean is keenly aware of how the entire organization must be focused on meeting the needs of the external customer to be successful.

But the word *customer* wasn't working for us because *customer* implies a need, and God needs nothing. The word *customer* does not begin to describe God's relationship toward all He has created.

This creates a pesky problem, because if God needs nothing why does He ask us for anything? If we have been given a gift for which there is no price, why do we even attempt to serve Him? In fact, if there is no compensatory relationship between Him and us, why don't we simply die at the moment of our conversion? To do so would surely save us a lot of trouble.

Other books have done a fine job of explaining why, once we have become believers, we do that which makes no practical sense from a human perspective. To go forward, let's accept that we have been created anew in Jesus Christ, we have a new heart and a new mind (2 Corinthians 5:17), and every fiber of our being ought to strive to please Him. To top it off, we have already been given far more than we deserve, which would be nothing! It is a reality that is impossible to fully understand until we are with Him in glory. As facile as English is, there is no single word to describe the mystery of why we serve Someone who has no needs. Our finite minds simply cannot conceive of taking an action that doesn't seek to achieve something better. But we must have a word with which to begin, and if *customer* does not work, it is the word *Lord* that we will use. We could use the words *Kurios* or *Adonai*, but they both mean *Lord* in another language. The English word *Lord* has an added benefit in that it is almost never used in American English except in reference to God Himself.

As we said earlier, some organizations do not have a clear understanding of why they do things. Because the church is stewarded by fallible people, it is no different. Sometimes those who lead and serve in the church get confused and end up focusing on the internal customers—the individual believers—and sub-optimize our internal performance when we should be looking at the big picture. The entire organization should be striving to satisfy our Lord by providing that which He values most highly. Paul put it this way in Galatians 1:10 (ESV): "For am I now seeking the approval of man, or of God? Or am I trying to please man? If I were still trying to please man, I would not be a servant of Christ." More times than we care to admit, we find ourselves serving the interests of our internal customer, man, rather than our Lord.

God's Greatest Value is His Own Glory

In a spiritual context, the limitations of language, whichever language it is, apply to the word *value* just as they do to the word *customer*. Value implies something that someone can use. If someone can use something, it implies that someone needs to use something. Someone who has no needs has no need of anything valuable. In fact, the word *value* becomes meaningless because it is a human term and is rooted in the practical nature of whatever we are talking about. There is no English word to fully describe something that is precious but has no instrumental value. We could use *desire* or *want,* but those are equally inadequate. But, for the sake of this discussion, we need a word to work with. Keeping in mind the shortcomings discussed above, we will continue to use *value*.

God's values must be understood based on inalienable truths found only in the Bible. These truths cannot be compromised or the church will not be the organ of transformation He has intended it to be. We must focus on what is most precious to His heart—that which He most highly values. In the context of Lean, value is what the customer is willing to pay for. But, as believers, we won't be paid

A Bridge to Somewhere

in a traditional sense; although we note God's gracious eternal rewards for the faithful; see Luke 6:35; Colossians 3:24; Hebrews 11:6; 2 John 1:8; Revelation 11:18.

God has strong feelings about what He wants. He is a practical and expedient being, and because He is omnipotent He always has the big picture in mind. He is neither capricious nor irresponsible, and He's not about wasting our time or His resources on activities that do not provide the results that He expects.

The Bible is full of strong statements as to what God wants and doesn't want. It tells us many of the things that He values. Among them are God-centeredness, submission, the fruit of the Spirit, sacrifice, and obedience. But He values obedience more than sacrifice (1 Samuel 15:22). How can we know where to start? To focus on all of them, at the same time, for all disciples, is impossible and counterproductive.

Learning about what God doesn't value can help us learn about what He does value. Amos 5:21-24 (NIV) says, "I hate, I despise your religious feasts; I cannot stand your assemblies. Even though you bring me burnt offerings and grain offerings, I will not accept them. Though you bring choice fellowship offerings, I will have no regard for them. Away with the noise of your songs! I will not listen to the music of your harps. But let justice roll on like a river, righteousness like a never-failing stream!" Micah 6:8 (NIV) says, "He has showed you, O man, what is good. And what does the LORD require of you? To act justly and to love mercy and to walk humbly with your God."

If God has no needs, and yet He leads us to do things, we must ask ourselves, as Aristotle did, what end point represents the culmination of all our actions? It can only be something as difficult for us to grasp as the nature of God Himself. It can only be something that is unique to God and is found nowhere in humanity. And it surely must be something other than simply *living well*.

God has many communicable attributes that we also possess. God's very image is reflected, albeit imperfectly, in us. We have emotions and rational thought. Because God has written His law, including the Ten Commandments, on our hearts, we understand the difference between right and wrong (Romans 2). We love and we hate. We grieve and we rejoice.

There are other ways in which we reflect God's image, but let's move to God's incommunicable character traits which we don't possess. The most notable of these is His limitless glory (Romans 11:36). It is the sum—the end point—of

59

all He has created, all that He is, and all that He will accomplish. Everything on earth and in heaven leads to God's glory and ought to be used for the sake of His glory. God's glory is an end unto itself; it is His greatest value, His very nature. God has created us, individually and corporately, to glorify Him (Romans 15:6). His glory is the highest purpose of our existence, and if we fail to bring Him glory we fail in the area of ultimate purpose. To fulfill that purpose we must have a relationship of sufficient intimacy with Him as our "customer" to understand that His greatest value is His own glory, how that glory is generated, and why it is important to Him.

The Value Stream is the Transformation Process

We are created to glorify God and delight in all He is by being transformed into the likeness of Jesus Christ (Philippians 2:5). Becoming more like Jesus Christ and providing that opportunity for others glorifies God; God's glory is the very reason for our existence. In being transformed into Jesus' image, we reflect His glory to Him and to the world around us. Sin deprives us of this ability (Romans 3:23), but salvation restores it—partially in the present (2 Corinthians 3:18) but fully in the future (1 John 3:2). All will be right with the world when all God has created is fully restored to its ability to fulfill His intentions. In the meantime, God is glorified as we become more like Jesus Christ. As we become more like Jesus, we also gain the ability to fulfill the destiny He has planned for us and to help others do the same.

He wants a total makeover for each of us—starting with our heart. There is a direct parallel between the secular value stream and our being transformed into the likeness of Jesus Christ. If we account for the limitations of English again, *value stream* becomes *transformation process*. God doesn't value us or love us more as we are transformed; He values us and loves us all equally from before time began. It is the *process* of transformation, also known as our sanctification, which glorifies Him. He derives great joy in seeing us incrementally conformed with Jesus Christ. Being the Creator of this win-win situation, God makes our lives more meaningful and rewarding the more we become like His Son (John 10:10).

To generate that glory, God has established an intentional process into which He calls all of His children. In *Natural Church Development*, Christian Schwarz talks about biotic principles that are hardwired into all of creation. If we submit to these principles, and work with them, we will be transformed. If we resist, we will stay as we are and suffer becoming irrelevant in this changing world—a bride in a hand-me-down gown.

The beginning of our transformation is the salvation experience by which one of God's children is changed into a new creature with a new nature; this is the basis for further change and development as a member of the Bride of Christ. God creates each of us with unique characteristics and gives us special gifts to accomplish His grand plan. Our unique origins, talents, and spiritual gifts make each disciple a very specialized creature, each distinct from all others (1 Corinthians 12). By making us this way, He leads each of us toward our special and unique destiny.

Jesus molded His disciples to be like Him by integrating four formative elements into their lives (Luke 6:40). We have taken Bill Hull's four-stage transformation model from his book *Jesus Christ, Disciplemaker* and slightly modified its form (shown in the graphic below) to demonstrate the Lean characteristics of flow and pull. The four elements are broadly focused, multifaceted, comprehensive, and indispensable. Like the secular value stream, the transformation process is a one-way street with each principle leading to the next in the sequence. We start as spiritual babies and progress to mature Christlikeness. If you expect to do it out of sequence or if you expect your disciples to do it out of sequence, the result will be inferior quality, sterility, and apathy. This results in defeated lives.

Many traditional, twenty-first-century churches neither design their ministries to include all four of these characteristics nor balance them as well as they ought. Without this structure, there is little incentive or encouragement for the individual disciple to flow from one stage to the next, which explains the difference in impact between the first-century church and the twenty-first-century church.

As church planters or leaders in an established church, we must remember that God has very specific intentions for this church. He wills that the church become a group of people who value His glory as He values His glory, and who seek it in their daily lives as mature, Christlike disciples.

Your ministry will be successful, as God defines success, and God will be glorified, if everything you do contributes directly to transforming disciples. You must design and implement your new ministry, or steward your existing ministry, to engage in those activities that directly transforma your disciples into the image of Christ – so they best reflect God's glory in all they do. Ministries that fail to see the disciple-making process as God sees it must be altered or eliminated. This is the one goal that matters and is essential to your task.

Stage 1—Come and See
(a newly planted seedling)

Figure 4.2

This is our initial discovery of the King and the nature of His kingdom. It is when we hear the good news of salvation by faith alone in Christ alone, and when the Holy Spirit speaks to our hearts and calls us to Himself (Ephesians 1). We understand the nature of salvation and the significance of confession and repentance. We are awakened to the realization that there is much more than we ever thought possible to this world and the next. In Jesus' ministry, this is the point at which He calls His first disciples, mentors them, and gives them time to reflect, evaluate, and decide (Matthew 4:12-17; Mark 1:14-15; Luke 4:14-44; John 1:35; 5:47).

Stage 2—Come and Follow Me
(having taken root and beginning to grow)

Figure 4.3

At this stage we have begun the transformation process and are being formed to live a kingdom life. We have experienced the miracle of new birth and are gaining strength; we are becoming like Jesus. Our spiritual horizons are expanding and others are beginning to notice the changes in us. Evil begins to react to us as we develop; we experience spiritual warfare for the first time (Matthew 4:18-25; Mark 1:16; 3:12; Luke 5:1; 6:11).

Stage 3—Come and Be with Me
(a mature tree bearing fruit)

Figure 4.4

Here we are equipped to harvest for the kingdom. We gain spiritual vigor and self-sufficiency, and begin practicing our faith. We begin to see the big picture and how it all fits together. As we see the promise more clearly, we mature and find a community of believers where we apply our spiritual gifts. Spiritual warfare increases and we recognize the magnitude of our stewardship and the consequences of our actions. Our relationship with God takes on an intensely personal character (Matthew 5:1; 25:46; Mark 3:13; 13:37; Luke 6:12; 21:38; John 6:1; 12:50).

Stage 4—Go and Make Disciples
(a mature tree bearing fruit and reproducing itself)

Figure 4.5

At this point our childhood is over and we begin a new phase of our relationship with Jesus—the phase in which we reproduce. Jesus has developed each of us and we receive the full extent of His love. We are ready to fulfill the Great Commission, to go unto all nations and testify what He has done in our lives. The fruit that we bear begins bearing its own fruit; we receive Jesus' blessing to become tools for exponential growth in both individuals and groups (Matthew 26:1; 28:20; Mark 14:1; 16:20; Luke 22:1; 24:53; John 13:1; 21:25).

By no means do we suggest that one must reach maturity in Christ prior to sharing the gospel with others. This is neither true nor helpful. We believe only that there is a normative process as a person moves from unbelief to maturity in the Lord. Neither do we deny a pre-stage that applies to many seekers and attenders who, for various reasons, come to church but are far from a personal relationship with the Lord. We rejoice that such people come, but our four stages start with those who are at the cusp of eternity, moving from unbelief to belief and acceptance of Christ.

The following graphic illustrates the four stages of transformation through which God intends each of His children to pass. Christ provides the *pull*. The local church should provide the *flow*.

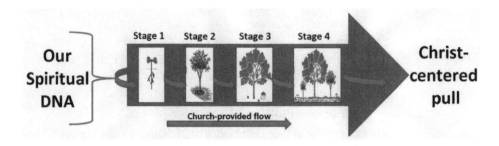

Figure 4.6: The Four Stages of Transformation

The Church Provides Flow for the Transformation Process

The job of the local church is to provide an environment in which the transformation of each individual disciple can flow in response to the pull of Jesus Christ and where each individual can develop and thrive. This will permit individual disciples to move from one stage to the next according to God's timing. Lean calls this *flow*.

To do this, the transformation process must have its characteristics tailored specifically to the people group at hand, accounting for extreme diversities mentioned earlier, to permit those disciples to flow from one stage in the transformation process to the next in response to the *pull* of Jesus Christ.

Unfortunately, the twenty-first-century church is not as good at doing this as we ought to be. Too often, we group people into batches. Processing large batches of anything is for the convenience of the processor, and not for the convenience of the customer or the quality of whatever is being processed. Batch processing in ministry results in trying to move people along at the same time, regardless of what their, or our Lord's, timelines are. Often, these batches of people don't go anywhere at all, but are overprocessed with the same treatment many times. The result is individual disciples stagnating in large, unusable inventories. Batch processing violates the principles of both secular and spiritual Lean, and brings flow to a halt.

Without an understanding of, and submission to, God's timing, there can be no transformation flow. The timing of the transformation of each believer is unique; each believer has his or her own *takt* timeline established by God. This timeline is established by the relationship between the individual and God, not by the relationship between the individual and the local church. Each disciple can develop only as fast as God's plan allows. But that development can be restricted by how the transformation process is stewarded.

In the present-day church, we have a bad habit of trying to make one size fit all. The most common form of this one-size-fits-all process is the weekly sermon to a large and diverse group. It too often serves as the only tool in the transformation process. We do not oppose corporate worship—it is clearly biblical—but it should not be the sole means by which disciples are being fed spiritually. It is possible that it should not be even the *main* means. One-on-one discipleship, smaller accountability groups, and other, more tailored means of transformation are indispensable. In our one-size-fits-all world we make some very bold and some very puerile presumptions.
- The first presumption is that all disciples have the same characteristics and have an equal ability to absorb the same material at the same time.
- Second, we presume that all disciples have the same spiritual *takt* time.
- Third, we presume that all disciples will make the same whistle-stops along the same path on their way to a common destiny.
- Fourth, we presume that God wants everything to happen the same way, and at the same time, for each believer.

Inductive reasoning tells us that, if we did not make these presumptions about our local church body, we would not structure our ministries with large groups being processed using a one-way transfer of common information all at the same time. In so doing we actually treat all disciples as if they were manufactured parts, each stamped from the same piece of sheet metal and formed by the same die to be used for the same purpose at the same time. This demonstrates arrogance in the extreme. Perhaps it is mandated by traditions, church structures, denominational expectations, and congregational expectations. In any case, it neither values the disciple as an individual nor glorifies God. Expecting the weekly sermon to be the primary means of disciple transformation is naïve, self-serving, and lazy. Jesus spent three and a half years as an itinerant rabbi living and sharing life with the disciples He transformed. Did they hear Jesus preach to multitudes? Yes! But they were also transformed by one-on-one time, one-on-three time, and one-on-twelve time with Jesus by living with Him and learning transformation firsthand.

No two disciples are the same. Neither are we all on the same timetable for development and deployment against the enemy. There are as many development timetables as there are disciples to develop, and these timetables are established by God. God has a unique *takt* time for each person He calls and for each one He will call in the future. To treat all disciples the same way, at the same time, using the same processes attempts to dumb God down to a shocking low. To think we can effectively or efficiently manage this through application of a modal, one-size-fits-all, transformation process is the height of folly. We are putting God in a box of our own design.

Without pull there can be no flow and without flow pull is useless. The believer can only flow from one stage to the next by responding to Jesus Christ, understanding how God's timing for his or her life applies at the moment, and moving with Jesus Christ to the next stage in his or her development, all this occurring at God's timing. It is the local church's job to understand this reality, structure these processes, and provide an environment for flow to take place.

Without understanding that the transformation process is deliberate, is incremental, transforms definable characteristics of a believer, and proceeds on a timeline unique to each individual, we will be guided by our own understanding, limited as it is, and steward the transformation process using methodologies of our own creation for our own convenience. At best, the transformation process will reach some level of entropy, resulting in transformation of individual disciples by accident, if at all. We end up using the greatest volume of our resources to accomplish the least impact. This does not glorify God. We must provide flow by accommodating the transformation of believers on an individual basis.

The Pull Comes from the Spirit of Jesus Christ

The shortest section of this chapter deals with what we hope is most self-evident: Jesus Christ, through His Spirit, pulls us to Himself (Ephesians 1). The pull of the Spirit of Jesus Christ is the dominant subject of the New Testament. Christ pulls us to Himself like a magnet each day and every day for all of our lives. He doesn't force us, but calls us kindly and firmly to follow Him and become like Him. Jesus' pull is what gives the disciple impetus to move through the process from one stage to the next. It is constant, indelible, and irrevocable. It simply is—because He is.

Jesus purposefully and continually pulls us to Himself and integrates the eight essentials of our spiritual DNA into lifelong transformation, enabling us to become and do that for which He created and redeemed us. He exerts this pull on all believers, but He does it on an individual basis.

As we flow through the transformation process we will find ourselves drawn closer to God and transformed into a closer resemblance to Christ, just as were Jesus' original disciples. As we are transformed, we will find ourselves becoming more like our Master and enjoying a relationship of deeper intimacy with Him.

Continuous Improvement of the Transformation Process

If Lean ministry's purpose is to identify and minimize waste in the transformation process, continuous God-centered improvement is the engine that drives it. The church cannot adapt to the changing and emerging needs of the world around it without a continuous improvement process in place. It behooves us to give some thought as to how we are going to improve what we do without compromising the truth of what we represent. If normative church leadership was asked to describe their transformation process and how they plan to improve it, many might shrug their shoulders and turn their palms up. This is exactly why the church needs Lean.

Jesus doesn't teach us how to deal with every complex situation that we might come across. He didn't give detailed instructions on how we should handle every situation in our lives. Instead, He teaches us principles that apply in many situations. While the principles never change, the circumstances in which the principles are applied change quickly and often.

The transformation process is not a once-and-for-all package to be executed in a static environment with a great many rules to accommodate any potentiality. It was designed by God as simple and open-ended. It was designed to be continually refined to glorify Him through our transformation (Philippians 2 and Colossians 1).

One is reminded of the excellent book—with a compelling title—by Patrick Lencioni, *Death by Meeting*. The authors of this book have been in, and have probably led, many meetings they felt would kill them—as have most of us! Attempting to improve by having constant meetings and busyness is seldom directly related to positive results in most organizations, including churches. God is intentional about all that He does. As imitators of God, His church should strive to be equally as intentional about monitoring, correcting, and adjusting the stewardship of ministries for maximum output—that output glorifying God through God-centered activities, as God intends—including improvements.

In today's church, improvements and changes are rightly vested with the church's leadership. It is the information gathering, problem analysis, and recommendation processes that need overhaul. Methods to get information from the people at ground level to the people who can make decisions are more or less nonexistent in today's church. We need a way to get feedback from the disciples who are journeying into greater intimacy with, and conformity to, the likeness of Jesus Christ into the hands of those who can implement improvements.

Local church leadership doesn't have all the answers to all the problems. What they have, through their congregations, is access to all the answers to all the problems. These are two very different things. Anyone in a leadership capacity who thinks he or she has all the answers is in the wrong job.

Improvements in the transformation process should not be solely dependent on either higher education or formal authority. By vesting responsibility for gathering information and implementing change with only the leadership of the church, we have imposed on them unrealistic expectations. The leadership needs to tap the resident strengths of its constituency.

A continuous improvement process requires the use of simple and easily measureable parameters to determine progress. The secular value stream contains simple measurements telling us how effective or efficient we are at managing it. The typical local church has no such ability to measure performance. Measuring the efficiency and effectiveness of the local church's transformation process doesn't sound difficult. But when one considers a congregation of two hundred to five hundred people, with each believer finding himself or herself in different and unique circumstances, and each being met in a unique way by God, the combination of what we could measure becomes complex in the extreme. Each believer is at a unique place on God's *takt* timeline and occupies a unique place within any of the four stages of transformation. It is no wonder we become overwhelmed and resort to bigger-is-better, one-size-fits-all indicators of transformation, and then move on to the really important things like, are we meeting our budget?

We should be focused on seeing God's purposes fulfilled by organizing ourselves and structuring what we do to be in sync with God's glorification and how that glorification is provided. It is uncomfortable, even impossible, for many people to grasp that the world changes around us even though the gospel does not. We must continue to change our processes, as our target changes, in order to accomplish our goal to develop Christlike disciples whose lives honor God and who can repeat the process with others. And we need to measure where we are at and whether we are moving forward or backward.

From time to time we take a survey, but they are most often very general in nature and there is seldom an overhaul of our transformation process until the church is mired deep in some sort of conflict, which can lead to an acrimonious split or worse, the death of a church. It is critical to Lean ministry implementation that the leadership receive continual input and evaluation of the church's performance from all those involved in the transformation process. This ensures the control and elimination of waste. Until such a continuous improvement process is in place, the church cannot hope to respond effectively to the postmodern culture around us.

CONVERGE WORLDWIDE—Orlando, FL
Cross-cultural Lean in Action

In late 2007, I was preparing to lead a leadership development and church mobilization effort with some of our Latino churches. Having recently learned about Lean, I sensed it would complement our process.

My perception was correct and I began to look at the vitally important "CUSTOMER"—even if God wasn't the traditional "customer." Latino churches place a high value on honoring God. But, like many, ours also struggled with the cultural tendency to unduly "honor people" by allowing human agendas, foibles, and preferences, rather than God's, to determine their priorities, perspectives, and practices. That had to change so our churches could change, too. But it would only change when we correctly saw God in His rightful role.

We did not approach the issue with a direct frontal assault on human leadership, but by looking at God (the "CUSTOMER") in Revelation 4 and 5. God's holiness, sovereignty, goodness, and grace combine to make those who live in His presence want—even long—to worship Him. When we really see Him, God is not only incomparable; He is irresistible. Then we worship Him for all He is and does with a joy that flows from hearts so moved by His absolute praiseworthiness that we can do nothing less. This worship becomes continual because we discover new reasons for it. Seeing God as He really is opens sin-blinded eyes to see the truth about Him and what He values more clearly. Small, human ambitions tend to be exposed for what they are.

God is far more than a human customer, but the parallel is still helpful. As the Beginning and the End, the One who is and stands at the Head of a process He has designed, He has initiated it and brings it to a culmination in Himself in a way that must exclude human agendas. His character, values, and purposes are the source as well as the goal of all effort to honor Him. He determines the design, standards, and expectations for the "product"—the transformation of disciples whom He is forming into the new humanity. This fully reflects His glory. He must be the One we seek to please, the One whose "Well done" we long to hear as a result of all we do.

I had an "Aha!" moment when Lean helped me to see clearly how the very nature of this divine "CUSTOMER" is the source of "pull" in the transformation process. As beings created in God's image, we are made to be like Him. Jesus stated the Lean principle of "pull" when He said in John 12:32, "I, when I am lifted up …will draw all men to myself." "Pull" results when we see Him as He is and we want to become as much like Him as possible. When we begin to see Him as He is, and to realize the depth to which sin has blinded us to the truth about Him, we are as naturally and progressively attracted to Him as the negative pole of a magnet is to the positive.

This "pull" stands in stark contrast to the "push" that characterizes ministry when we do not see God as He is and are motivated by guilt, spiritual blackmail, intimidation, fear, or obligation. This kind of "pull" is the motivation that the people in our churches need.

– Eric Johnson
Director of Latino Ministries
Converge Worldwide

5

Chapter

Deconstructing Our Spiritual DNA

"Life! You hear me!?
Give my creation life!
…

Alive! It's alive! It's alive!"

— Young Frankenstein 1974,
Gene Wilder and Mel Brooks

Our journey of transformation occurs in three tenses: past, present, and future. The past tense deals with our deliverance from the penalty of sin (Romans 6:23; 8:1) This is our *justification* provided by Christ on the cross. The future tense deals with deliverance from the presence of sin (Revelation 22). This is our *glorification* provided by God in heaven.

But the present tense deals with our deliverance from the power of sin in our daily lives (Romans 12:1-2) This is our personal *sanctification* or ongoing transformation. Many churches neglect the present tense in practice. They function as if salvation had only two stages—past and future; as if it only offered forgiveness and heaven, and not much in between. Such neglect occurs when churches don't realize that the second stage is an equally important piece of the process. Healthy churches correct this deficiency by functioning with a complete gospel. A gospel that only invites people to receive the forgiveness of Jesus as Savior, but not to become like Him, is an incomplete gospel producing defeated lives and sterile churches. We are called to "work out our salvation with fear and trembling" (Philippians 2:12 NIV). This does not mean we can save ourselves through good works, which is impossible according to Ephesians 2:8-9, but rather that the evidence of true saving faith always results in good works (Ephesians 2:10). This is the clear teaching of James (2:14-26) where he says that true faith always results in God-centered works.

If you have given your life to Christ, and you are not dead, you are living in the present tense of the salvation experience. You are living in the growth tense, the transformation tense. You are the Body of Christ. You are the church.

The church's mission is to provide all believers the opportunity for spiritual transformation to take place (Colossians 1:28-29). Second Corinthians 3:18 is pivotal when it says, "And we all, with unveiled face, beholding the glory of the Lord, are being transformed into the same image from one degree of glory to another. For this comes from the Lord who is the Spirit" (ESV). Spiritual transformation is key to bringing glory to God; He is glorified as we are conformed more and more to His image.

To provide the opportunity for spiritual transformation we must promote the development of healthy, fruitful churches equipped to reach the next generation, both in the U.S. and abroad. But the dizzying array of people groups waiting to be transformed can be overwhelming. This complexity is further compounded by the fact that each believer is a unique creature and has a unique spiritual *takt* time and is purposed by God for a particular journey (1 Corinthians 12:12-26).

So, with all this uniqueness distributed throughout the world, we must define those most basic elements that are common to all believers. We realize this may spark some heated theological debates. But this is not the forum for engaging theological and denominational intricacies. We are simply saying that commonalities exist across the board within God's Kingdom, no matter what external characteristics are manifest. Before we go into the details of our spiritual DNA we must understand what cannot be compromised.

The Barna Group lists eight elements that we consider to be nonnegotiable for a believer. They call it a "Biblical Worldview" and summarize it thusly:
1. Jesus Christ lived a sinless life.
2. God is the all-powerful and all-knowing Creator of the universe and He still rules it today.
3. Salvation is a gift from God and cannot be earned.
4. Satan is real.
5. A Christian has a responsibility to share his or her faith in Christ with other people.
6. The Bible is accurate in all of the principles it teaches.
7. Unchanging moral truth exists.
8. Such truth is defined by the Bible.

We believe that acceptance of these baseline truths is necessary for all believers. To deny any of them is to invite perversion of what God has defined as truth. Once having accepted these eight baseline elements, we can go on to understand the commonalities within the believers' DNA and how those commonalities have indispensable implications to minimizing waste and creating healthy churches that can minister effectively throughout the world—to all people groups.

Many who have accepted salvation through faith in Christ alone (Titus 3:3-10) remain spiritually stunted because the church fails to promote what God wants and even demands: the process of lifelong transformation of our spiritual DNA. We believe this is the foundational issue that church planters and existing churches must address personally, intentionally, and biblically in order for their lives, their gospel, and their ministry to truly be *Good News*.

In our Western culture we have a propensity to present two versions of the transformation process, both of which hide the big picture of how God is creating a new humanity in Christ. One says, "This is how you do it. You must always do it this way because we have a clear understanding of what will work and what won't work and if you do it differently you will be doing it wrong."

The other says, "Just do whatever the Spirit leads you to do. He'll guide you to where He wants you to be and you'll be doing whatever God thinks is necessary."

There is some validity to each of these approaches, but neither of them accounts for both the diversity and the commonality within God's Kingdom. Until we have an understanding of how we are diverse and common at the same time, we will not be able to focus our efforts while minimizing waste. Either of these approaches is guaranteed to produce a race of believers with stunted spiritual DNA, causing them to live in isolation from their greater community and fail to achieve the potential assigned them by God. A church like this will not look like an Acts 2-type church.

Many people espouse the belief that we should become "like the first-century church." What exactly does that mean? You might say, "They wore funny clothes and had funny customs and women couldn't own property or have a job. They didn't have a vaccine for polio and they didn't have the Internet—they didn't even have indoor plumbing! We're not like them." Without identifying the commonalities between then and now, the idea of "becoming like the first-century church" can be very confusing.

Only when we understand what is being transformed can we become more, and live more, like Him—whatever century we live in. Only then will we be able to delight in Him and His purposes to the degree that fully glorifies Him and fully satisfies us. Humankind is only fully satisfied when our satisfaction comes from abiding in Christ and loving Him—this is the abundant life Christ spoke about in John 10:10. But when our transformation process loses this bigger picture, it produces defective spiritual DNA. It produces Christians who have little desire to grow in, and to serve, God, and who see little reason to connect with a local body to make an impact on our world. Only by recovering and implementing a transformation process focused on the biblical DNA resident in each believer can we generate seed capable of bearing biblical fruit.

We believe the Bible indicates beyond any reasonable doubt that there are discrete identifiable characteristics that are common to all re-born believers. Why common to all? We all have the same DNA because we all have the same Parent and through salvation are part of the same gene pool.

We grouped these characteristics into eight categories that we believe transcend time and space and have been goals of the transformed believer since time began.

Spiritual DNA

It is our spiritual DNA that is transformed. Embedded in and infused throughout the four stages of transformation discussed earlier are eight elements forming the spiritual DNA of each believer. They are:

- Education
- Evangelism and Missions
- Fellowship
- Prayer
- Service / Compassion
- Stewardship
- Wisdom
- Worship

We believe these eight basic elements are common to all believers who have lived, are living, or will live in the future. These are the identifiable characteristics of each believer that make up the essence of Christ in us and look more like Jesus Christ as we mature in Him.

We believe it is God's intention for each of His children to become fully developed in each of the eight elements of the spiritual DNA. This is a lifelong, never-ending process—the process of sanctification. Like the secular Lean value stream, the spiritual transformation process develops us from reflecting little or none of God's glory to the point where we reflect great glory for our Lord. How fully we develop depends on our willingness to submit ourselves to His guidance and leadership.

Most often we experience this development in the form of many successive, little changes rather than overnight metamorphoses. Like the value stream, the transformation process progresses in a linear fashion, each of the four stages sequentially preparing us for further refinement. To do so, God uses the tools He has available at the time, including the circumstances in which we find ourselves, to accomplish these changes. Some of the tools at His disposal are socioeconomic status, age, gender, the problems we deal with on a daily basis, culture, language, level of education, our intimate relationships, and other conditions and problems unique to each believer. The willingness and the ability of the local church to accommodate each believer, wherever that believer is on God's *takt* timeline of transformation, will determine the ratio of value to waste in the transformation of those believers.

Insomuch as a two-dimensional graphic can communicate something so profound, we think our spiritual DNA structure looks something like the one shown below. At the epicenter is Jesus Christ associated with a believer at the most intimate level, with each element of our spiritual DNA available to be touched by Him and transformed.

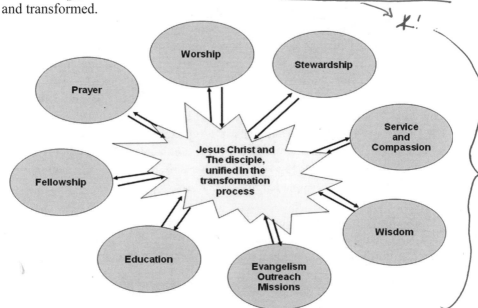

Figure 5.1: Spiritual DNA

Although these basic elements are common to all disciples, each element will take on secondary characteristics specific to different people and people groups and will manifest itself outwardly with diverse appearances. What we do will not change, but *how* we do it will.

Transformation of our spiritual DNA is not necessarily linear. It can begin anywhere, with one or more elements, depending on the personality characteristics God gave us. We each have personality characteristics that lend themselves to some elements more than others. We each have at least one spiritual gift that God intends to use for His glory and our edification (1 Corinthians 12, 14). Although our spiritual gifts will initiate more development in certain elements, we can start with any element—or multiple elements—all of which require development in all believers to some degree. First Timothy 4:6-10 uses the Greek word *gymnazo*, from which we derive the word *gymnastics*, to describe the hard work, sweat, and effort needed to develop good doctrine demonstrated in education and wisdom; and good discipline demonstrated in worship, stewardship, service, compassion, evangelism, outreach, missions, fellowship, and prayer. Transformation does not simply happen; we must "work out our salvation with fear and trembling" (Philippians 2:12 NIV).

Education

Patterned after the teaching-heavy ministry of Jesus Himself, the evangelical church in the twenty-first century focuses almost entirely on teaching—teaching from the pulpit, teaching in Sunday school, and teaching in small groups. So we could consider the education of Christian disciples as first among equals of the eight elements of our spiritual DNA. If the education of disciples is the basis for the other seven elements, we had better do it as effectively and efficiently as possible. No ministry, or other responsible organization whose primary goal is learning, would allow their students a completely self-directed or unguided approach to development represented by the one-size-fits-all methodology in place in most of our churches today. In large part, we do not use incremental courses of study with one topic leading to another.

Lifelong Christian education is necessary for healthy spiritual transformation (Psalm 119). Most often this is considered to be Bible study, be it self-study or in a group setting. But it is actually a much broader discipline involving Scripture memorization, Bible history and our heritage, and music education and its role in worship. It involves reading contemporary Christian literature and seeing Christian movies and attending seminars that explain the origin of our DNA and how it is relevant to the changing world around us. It includes an 8,000-odd-year heritage of where we came from, who we are, and where we are going as a people.

We will use a secular example here to illustrate how important it is to know who we are as a people. The average person on the street in the U.S. South knows much more about the U.S. Civil War, or the War Between the States, than do even well-read historians in the North. Southerners are often accused of living in the past and refusing to give up what happened generations ago. It is a cheap accusation because it has nothing to do with living in the past. Southerners know more about that period of U.S. history because those dark years defined who they are as a people through the terrible suffering they endured both during and after the War. It's important to them so they know about it. We Northerners blow it off because we didn't suffer that badly and we tend not to acknowledge how the Civil War defined us as a people or a nation. In his acclaimed documentary *The Civil War* Ken Burns claims that, as a defining moment in U.S. history, our Civil War has no equal. It was more formative than any other event our country has experienced.

To draw the obvious parallel, the history of Israel as conveyed in the Old Testament defines very much of whom we are as a people. Our legal, judicial, social, and governmental systems, many of our religious traditions, and most of the freedoms we take for granted as having been invented in the U.S. actually have their roots in the Old Testament. This should provide Christians with a homogenous identity—if we take the time to learn it—but it requires that we use the resources available to us and take the time to teach it. It is a part of the church's role to provide those resources and time. We spend much of our effort identifying and dwelling on the things that separate us as Christians, rather than the things that identify us as belonging to a unified people group.

When many of us were young our only educational resources were Sunday school, Vacation Bible School, and the occasional filmstrip. Today we have educational tools that most of us never dreamed possible. Today we have sophisticated audio/visual resources, the Internet, books on tape, and Christian movies. We have smart classrooms and, most of all, we have educated, experienced, and willing education professionals sitting in the pews. It is naive in the extreme to attempt to teach the entire volume of material we need to learn from the pulpit on Sunday morning. The Sunday sermon is good and valuable indeed, but we need other venues for learning.

The abundance of Christian literature on the market today is impressive. True, much of it isn't so good—it seems as if anyone can get a book published these days—but much of it is informative and edifying for Christians trying to live in today's world. We do not have a recommended reading list and it would be beyond the scope of this book to compile one here.

Moreover, we have never seen a church or denominational recommended reading list that is tied to stages of the development or transformation in their members. What the individual believer reads is solely at his or her discretion. We mean no implication that we should force our members to read certain materials. Rather that we might compile a list of Christian literature by category and by timeline and strongly *encourage* them to read it in proper sequence.

Excellent examples of reading lists separated by category of development are those used by all our U.S. Military Secretaries which are integral to the development of their members. It is categorized by rank and intended to be part of that service member's professional development. It comes in the form of fiction and non-fiction. It examines turning points in world history represented by specific battles and political sea changes. It examines different ideologies and systems and compares them to our own. It gives the member an understanding of history and its relevance and is part of each member's annual performance evaluation. Indeed, churches have libraries filled with relevant books but some never tap this important source—let alone firmly encourage it.

Even more so than good Christian books, the Bible should be central to our Christian education. It is the authority for our lives (2 Timothy 3:16-17). To be fully transformed Christians we must understand and embrace a biblical worldview, and to embrace a biblical worldview we must know what the Bible says about a wide range of issues. The biblical literacy of this generation is nowhere near what it was twenty-five, fifty, or a hundred years ago.

Who educated you in biblical principles? Who educates you today? How will you pass this knowledge on to succeeding generations? We need to be saturated in biblical truth, including a healthy dose of historical theology. To be transformed requires that we have an understanding of our common origins, pathways, and goals and that we minimize the superficial differences represented by our individual churches and denominations—the window-dressings that unfortunately so often divide brothers and sisters in Christ.

Worship

Worship is an act of submission to a higher power. In the case of true believers, this higher power is the one true God. He is the Highest Power in existence—the uncaused cause. Worship is formal acknowledgment of the attributes of God including His holiness, omnipotence, omniscience, omnipresence, goodness, and righteous wrath. Worship is extolling the virtues of God. Worship acknowledges that we cannot be our own god. It occurs once initially, and then daily, as we continue to pick up our cross and follow Him until that time when we are finally with Him in glory (Matthew 16:24). At that time we will truly worship Him with unadulterated joy (Revelation 4–5). In the present tense of our sanctification, worship occurs in a number of forms, both corporate and individual. It may happen during a Sunday morning service or it may happen during a time of meditation and solitude. We may worship during rush hour in a metropolitan area or we may worship alone in a remote area. Worship may include fasting (Matthew 6). Worship should be combined with prayer. Worship involves confession of our continuing sinful behaviors (I John 1:1:9), even though there is no future condemnation for believers (Romans 8:1), and constant, growing submission to God (Romans 7). Worship includes repentance stemming from the Hebrew word *shuv* and from the Greek word *metanoia* which both mean to turn away from sin and towards the Lord.

Worship is an activity critical to the transformation of the disciple. Worship places God in His rightful place and us in ours. Psalms 146–150 are excellent examples of worship. David extols the virtues of God; in detail he describes God's attributes and what He does with them. The word praise appears thirty-five times in the fifty-nine verses that comprise these five short chapters. David describes God to God Himself, and in so doing, describes himself as a man. He says God is:

- A builder
- A frustrater of the wicked
- A gatherer
- A giver
- A granter of peace
- A healer
- A helper
- A lifter
- A lover
- A provider

- A satisfier

- A delighter
- A sender of His word
- A strengthener
- A supplier
- A sustainer
- A watcher
- An understander
- An upholder
- Splendor
- The maker of heaven and earth and everything in them
- The namer of the heavens

Music is often not given its proper measure of respect as an element of worship. Music comes in many forms—both traditional and non-traditional. Martin Luther said, "I wish to see all arts, principally music, in the service of Him who gave and created them. I would not for all the world forego my humble share of music. Singers are never sorrowful, but are merry, and smile through their troubles in song. Music makes people kinder, gentler, more staid and reasonable. I am strongly persuaded that after theology there is no art that can be placed on a level with music; for besides theology, music is the only art capable of affording peace and joy of the heart." That's a strong statement from the man who was used by God in a powerful way to formally start the Protestant Reformation in 1517. Perhaps we should give a little more credence to his thoughts on the subject of music as worship. It really doesn't matter what kind of music works in your environment. Any music that authentically lifts our hearts in praise of God is acceptable. Anything that unites us together in worship is fine—all the way from heavy metal rock to a formal choir and a 1,000-pipe organ. You may disagree with this statement, but keep in mind the importance of our similarities don't get hung up on the secondary, divisive issues, such as the particular style of music used in worship.

Let us illustrate, by contrast, a couple of non-traditional ways we submit to something greater than ourselves and how deeply they can move and unite us. Indulge us for the next few paragraphs; relax your mind and let yourself drift. Become Walter Mitty. Imagine with us.

Imagine you find yourself as a member of a military convoy. You're no one special—just another small person in a very big world. The convoy is large and consists of many vehicles parked end-to-end stretched out for a mile or so. It may be comprised of tanks, trucks, armored personnel carriers or a mixture of all of them—it doesn't matter. The engines are silent and the soldiers mill around doing what soldiers do—they wait. It seems that they have been waiting for a long time. They smoke; they joke; they play catch and cards; many sleep. It is hot and everyone is dirty and impatient. All is idle.

And then, from the command vehicle, the order comes to mount up and the drivers start their engines. The order runs the length of the convoy like a high-speed fuse, and in an eye blink all that idleness becomes action going in all directions. The engines start and the men collect their gear and scramble for their positions. The drivers rev the engines to make sure they are running properly. The noise of the shouting and the sound of many engines displaces all but your private thoughts.

As the crescendo of what is happening around you builds, and the convoy begins to move, you are suddenly swept with a deep emotion that you cannot control. You are immobilized in your small place and at the instant of movement you strangely feel like bursting into tears. You are shocked and embarrassed as you struggle to control it. You cast a sidelong glance at the man sitting next to you and are taken aback to see tears rolling down his cheeks. What is happening? You are outside yourself and looking in at someone else. And that person is behaving strangely.

Cut away, Walter, to another place. You find yourself standing on the steel deck of a naval warship. The ship has just left the pier and is being towed toward the open sea. Leaving your wife and children on the pier was hard; it was very hard. It was a sad thing and you are in pain. But soon you will be at sea and you have work to do. You turn to your tasks.

As the ship clears the breakwater the towing warps are cast off and the tugs fall away. The order goes to the engine room to make steam and increase turns on the screws. The ship responds and suddenly it is a living thing beneath your feet with a soul of its own. There is very little sound, but the vibrations from her power plant come up through the deck into your feet. They move up through your groin and swell into your chest. Outside the breakwater the ship picks up the rhythm of the sea around her and rides up, down, and through the waves. In those few short minutes your world is transformed and your heart soars! The emotion of what happened on the pier is replaced by a rogue wave of feeling crashing over you so strong as to take your breath away.

As before, you are so deeply and strangely moved that you fear it and recoil. You look around and see that others feel the same. The level of energy is palpable. Each deals with it in his own way—but it's the same for all. Some busy themselves at their work with heads down; some joke about it; others are simply silent. The Captain, sitting in his bridge chair with seat belt fastened and feet braced against the bulkhead, stares straight ahead—the vise of his jaw holding an unlit cigar. His eyes are dry behind dark glasses as he vainly tries not to communicate what all around him are feeling. But he is belied by his stoicism.

What was it you were feeling in these situations, Walter? Was it fear? Was it anger or sadness? No, it was none of these. What you were feeling was joy. You have feelings of unbounded joy at being part of something so much bigger than your insignificant self, something so big that your individual worth is eclipsed by the greatness of the effort around you. You are feeling the joy of being part of a community much greater than the sum of its individual parts.

The sound of the diesel engines, the vibration of the living ship underneath you, and the rhythm of the sea spoke to you in a language that touched the totality of yourself and everything around you and spoke deep into your human soul. It took you outside yourself and loosed powerful emotions that were lying dormant inside you—feelings that you didn't even know you had. In the moments described above you realized your purpose was clarified within a greater community. You became small and great all in the same instant.

Holy worship is knowing that our purpose has been clarified as a part of a God-exalting community much greater than ourselves—and focused on an infinite Being endlessly greater than ourselves! To grow and be truly transformed requires that we worship God daily in all the forms He has made available to us. This is what Paul conveys when he bursts forth in Romans 11:33 with, "Oh, the depth of the riches and wisdom and knowledge of God! How unsearchable are his judgments and how inscrutable his ways" (ESV). When we praise God for who He truly is, we truly know God and truly make Him known. Worship is part of our spiritual DNA.

Prayer

First Thessalonians 5:17 instructs us to "pray without ceasing" (ESV). But is prayer monologue or is it dialogue? If it's monologue, what's the point? If prayer is dialogue, how does God respond to our communication? For those predeterminists in the crowd—if God already knows the outcome of everything He has created and set in motion, what's the point of praying? He's got it all worked out. If He doesn't have it all worked out, His immutability comes into question. For many of us on the far side of the pulpit, prayer is confusing. We are told if our faith is as large as a mustard seed we will be granted all that we ask. Check out a mustard seed next time you open a jar of sweet pickles. A mustard seed is very small. So we pray and sometimes our requests are granted and sometimes they are not.

Sometimes it is a bitter experience when our requests are not granted. Loved ones languish and die. Fortunes are lost. Children stray off the path. This puts us in a bit of a pickle (pun intended). If God knows best, why does He ask us to pray? It couldn't simply be to make Him feel good because God doesn't need us to make Him feel good.

Prayer is not as simple as it sounds. Its physiology, purpose, response, and timing are complex, and we challenge the reader to recall a time when you had the physiology of prayer broken down from the pulpit. Dr. Jeff Hinds is a seminary-trained pulpiteer who freely admits that the thought of breaking down the physiology of prayer is intimidating.

We spend a lot of time asking God to do things for us. But God is not a genie in a bottle that exists to make our every wish come true. Many times His answer is "No." and we should praise Him for that answer as well. The essence of prayer is not getting God to do things for us. It is something much bigger than that. Prayer cannot be explained by platitudes like, "Prayer changes us." That may be true—in fact it certainly is true—but such an explanation isn't enough when we stake the most intimate needs of our being on prayer. Yet He still urges us to pray. Therefore prayer must have a much grander nature than we casually assume.

Prayer can be corporate, solitary, verbal, non-verbal, liturgical, in tongues, conversational, and sometimes even raging at God as did David. It comes as an activity combined with meditation, solitude, and fasting (Matthew 4). For those who have trouble stringing together a coherent series of thoughts or words without being interrupted by the need to adjust your hair, make a phone call, or check your e-mail, there is prayer journaling.

Yet who taught you to pray? Who was your prayer mentor? If prayer is as important as the Bible indicates, what makes us think it will simply happen? If it's so important, should we not be given detailed instruction in the area of prayer—how, when, and what for? We've all heard it said that the perfect prayer was modeled for us by Jesus when He prayed the Lord's Prayer in the Sermon on the Mount (Matthew 6). But we can't just repeat that over and over again, can we—or can we? Perhaps not—for Jesus didn't say, "When you pray, pray this…" (Matthew 6:9). Instead He said, "Pray then *like* this" (Matthew 6:9 ESV, emphasis added). The Lord's Prayer is a model to follow rather than words to lifelessly repeat.

God doesn't give us everything we ask for simply because He does have everything under control—in contrast to you and me. To give us everything we foolishly ask for would undermine His best in our lives because we often "ask wrongly, to spend it on our passions" (James 4:3 ESV). Often, our prayers fall impotent to the ground because we ask while harboring unresolved sin within our hearts (Psalm 66:18; Proverbs 28:9) or we ask without an attitude of faith (James 1:6-7). Our Lord delights in answering our prayers when we ask for God-centered things, with God-centered hearts. We often lose out on such God-centered blessings simply because we do not know how to ask (James 4:2). Our local churches must teach us to pray—not simply expect us to pray.

Stewardship

Through our relationship with God the Father, and the intercession of Jesus Christ His Son, we have been given wealth beyond understanding. Even the poorest believer among us is wealthy (Ephesians 1:3). But stewardship is most often discussed solely in a financial context. True, it is important that we support our ministries with our financial gifts (2 Corinthians 8–9), but that is only a part of stewardship when in the larger context. Stewardship involves *everything* God has given us, not just our money. He's given us time and talents to secure ourselves as God-sufficient in a demanding world. Such time and talents are always to be used for His glory. He's also given each of us at least one spiritual gift intended to be used for His glory and the furtherance of His kingdom (1 Corinthians 12:7). To some He's given the ability to effectively manage the Kingdom's resources, including financial and material resources.

The average congregation in the U.S. has much to give in the form of both money and talent. We are considered to be the wealthiest country in the world. But sermons on giving of our finances are rare because they are feared to be offensive, especially to unbelievers—"All the church wants is my money." But giving our finances to God's work establishes a relationship between Him and us regarding our material resources that cannot be established if our wallet squeaks when we open it (2 Corinthians 8–9). God owns it all. We just use His resources, entrusted to us, for a time. It is important that we, as believers, have a working understanding of this biblical principle.

A professional cross-section of any average congregation would show an array of talents capable of responding to just about any need. We have people who can make things, teach things, heal things, grow things, and cook things. Stewardship should be a supporting discipline to several other elements of spiritual DNA—among them, service and compassion, education, and evangelism and missions. People in the U.S. are retiring earlier and living longer. Should we not view that leisure time as a gift from God to support His Kingdom? Or should we just say, "Thank you very much, God," and use it for our own vain pursuits? What a waste of time. An excellent text on this subject is John Piper's *Don't Waste Your Life*.

Who wants to face the Father having had the goal of showing Him how perfect our golf swing became during the last third of our lives? Or who wants to relate all the game shows we watched during our final-chapter years when we could have used the time He entrusted to us for glorious purposes? No thanks! We need to develop an understanding that we must use our time wisely—it's all His time and we just use it for a season.

There's a reason why the widow's two mites were more highly regarded than the larger, casual gifts of the multitudes—even though her gift totaled only one-fourth of a penny (Mark 12:41–44). Jesus was thrilled because she had a more intimate relationship with God than did the multitudes, demonstrated by giving all that she had. We have so much more, yet our devotion to the Lord is often so much less.

As we said, stewardship is not just about time, talent, and money. For many of us, the most precious resources we have are the people God has given us and our relationships with them. We have our husbands, wives, and children. We have our extended families. We exist in a three-dimensional world of relationships with people above, below, and on all sides of us. Other than the death of Christ for our sins, this is the most precious gift of all. Through devoted stewardship we must nurture each other and teach those believers who are less mature how to steward all they have, including money, time, talents, and relationships for His glory.

Our judgment at the *bema* seat of Christ will be based on what we did with what we were given while here on earth—all of what we were given (1 Corinthians 3:10–15; 2 Corinthians 5:10). While there is no condemnation for believers in Christ (Romans 8:1), there will be gracious rewards for the faithful (1 Corinthians 3:14). From those who have been given more, more will be required (Luke 12:48). When that day comes, all of us want to be able to stand tall and hear Jesus say, "Well done, good and faithful servant" (Matthew 25:21 ESV). God's people need to understand the principle of stewardship in order to be transformed, and good stewardship brings glory to God as it demonstrates the utter dependence of the created on the Creator.

Wisdom

Wisdom is mentioned over 200 times in the Bible (215 times in the NIV). The Bible defines wisdom as "the fear of the LORD" (Proverbs 1:7 NIV). This means that whenever we condition our actions, thoughts, motives, attitudes, and activities to please the Lord, we have acted wisely and put our Christianity into practice. But if we take a closer look at the biblical definition we see that wisdom is demonstrated insight into complex spiritual issues and an ability to bring Scripture to bear on practical situations helping guide broken people towards God's healing grace. Wisdom is guidance from a position of superior Scriptural understanding; wisdom is mentoring those who need development; wisdom does the right thing instead of doing things right; Bible-centered leadership and wisdom go hand-in-hand; wisdom incorporates justice, reward, and discipline based on an unchanging standard;

wisdom is applied leadership in a practical way to move both the Body and the individual through the transformation process; the presence or absence of wisdom is one of the litmus tests of God-centered leadership.

We don't talk much about wisdom, not even in the church. Perhaps we think it is clearly understood in our time. Again, we challenge the reader to recall a time when this element, wisdom, was dismantled and examined—element by element—from the pulpit. God considers wisdom worthy of our aspirations because He graciously tells us that He'll give us wisdom if we ask for it by faith: "If any of you lacks wisdom, he should ask God, who gives generously to all without finding fault, and it will be given to him" (James 1:5 NIV).

Wisdom is an element of our spiritual DNA worthy of significant attention considering the conflicting value systems extant in our world today, each with its own definition of "truth" and "right". In the case of orthodox Christianity, wisdom presupposes an origin from a standard greater than ourselves—wisdom is from God.

If Christian wisdom is based on God's truth, and if it is always centered on what pleases God more than anything else, then true wisdom will allow Christians to successfully navigate life. The Godly Christian is a wise Christian, and such wisdom speaks directly to a previous example—biblical education. No one can be wise in the eyes of God without knowing God's Word and then living out God's Word with a full desire to please Him.

Wisdom is most often considered the domain of the elder members of the church. But nowhere does God say that we have to be old, or be a church officer, to be wise. Wisdom is also gender non-specific. Paul's letter to Titus is a model of the development and distribution of wisdom through mentorship. In chapters 1 and 2 Paul defines a hierarchy of mentorship beginning with himself. He is Titus's mentor. He doesn't give Titus's age, but he calls him "my true son" (v. 4 NIV); indicating that perhaps Titus was junior to Paul in age. Titus is to initiate the mentorship program in Crete. The Cretans, true to their name, have been acting badly. Titus is to proliferate Paul's wisdom and mentorship beginning with the older men, to whom he is probably a junior. Paul gives Titus a number of cautions so that he will maintain credibility in the group. The older men are to serve as examples to the younger men (2:2). Titus is then to go on to the older women who, in turn, serve as examples to the younger women (Titus 2:3–5). Then he is to train the young men to whom he is most likely a peer (2:6–8). This will be tough for Titus, and Paul asks him to set a personal example. Paul finishes by instructing Titus to teach the slaves to be above reproach in all that they do so through all their behaviors they will make "the teaching about God our Savior attractive" (2:10). The result is a closed-loop model of mentorship involving all gender and socioeconomic strata.

Considering the implications of the paragraphs above we think the church should be very heavily focused on the deliberate development of wisdom in its members through mentorship, starting with a spiritual gifts discovery course to determine those whom God has so gifted. But too often this is left to chance. Who was your mentor? Did anyone teach you wisdom? Many believers have not, do not, and will never have a mentor. How would you, the elder and more experienced member, feel being mentored by someone your junior? Most would not be able to humble themselves in this vertical relationship, even though our younger members are the future of the church, have answers to many of the church's problems, and are asking questions which older members are not.

Recently a good friend told us that he keenly felt the absence of a mentor. We were surprised because this is a godly man of significant strength and conviction who lives his life and guides his actions by biblical principles. He is defined by what Paul says about deacons and elders in 1 Timothy 3 and is someone we should all emulate. He is also sixty-three years old. What would he possibly want a mentor for? Yet he expressed a lifelong need to have someone senior to him in the faith come alongside him and provide continuing guidance. He needs a mentor as we all need mentors. We are hardwired to have someone nurture us. That need doesn't go away with age. In addition, we should all be mentors, developing wisdom in those who have less spiritual maturity than we.

Wisdom isn't acquired overnight. It is developed over time and it generally involves pain combined with a minimum of self-deception. It may come to a younger person or maybe an older person, but it takes biblical knowledge, time, and seasoning through experience. We have to put those life experiences into the context of Christian principles. We must honestly assess what we did right and wrong before we can hope to execute biblical wisdom in the face of real pain and suffering in our lives and those of others. Are we capable of mentoring? Are we mentoring anyone? Do we have a mentor to help us develop wisdom? The answers to these questions are: Yes, we are; we should be; and we should have one. It's a necessary part of our DNA as a believer.

Fellowship

The word "fellowship" is mentioned ninety-six times in the Bible, eighty-four of them combined with the word "offering" (NIV). The word "offering" implies a number of things: vertical separation of the parties involved; worship; forgiveness, which, in turn, implies sin; repentance; developmental spirituality; and ministry through practicality. Christian fellowship is something deeper than sharing a meal or a Saturday on the lake fishing with your Christian brethren.

In this case, Webster's definition won't do. The best he can come up with is, "a community of interest, feeling, communion, as between members of the same church." It's okay, but just a little too simple for what we are trying to communicate. What the Bible is talking about is something much deeper and interconnected. Biblical fellowship, or *koinonea*, is a community of God-honoring persons, having deep biblical convictions, which share each other's pain and suffering and who strengthen each other and sacrifice for one another.

The Bible requires us to fellowship with two groups of people. The first group is made up of believers. Fellowship with those inside the Body serves many purposes. It affirms our place in God's Kingdom and reinforces who we are and what we are about. It strengthens each of us in a way that is impossible in solitude. Our relationship with each other is a physical representation of our relationship to Jesus Christ and the Holy Spirit (1 Corinthians 1:9; 2 Corinthians 13:14). It allows us to share in Christ's sufferings together (Philippians 3:10). The apostle John said, "We proclaim to you what we have seen and heard, so that you also may have fellowship with us. And our fellowship is with the Father and with His Son, Jesus Christ" (1 John 1:3). Fellowship provides an opportunity for us to minister to each other even as Jesus ministered to Simon's mother-in-law (Mark 1:29–31). Fellowship provides an opportunity to teach each other (Mark 10:34–45). Fellowship provides an opportunity to turn love into action (John 21:15–22). It is impossible to have healthy spiritual DNA without fellowship with the Body.

The second group with which we are to fellowship are those who are not yet followers of Christ. Fellowship is possible with the second group, but not to the extent that exists among fellow believers. We must respond differently to each group. In *The Forgotten Ways*, Alan Hirsch discusses in detail the need for us to live in limnality with the unbelieving world around us. By that he means in contact with or side-by-side with them. We can't sequester ourselves away and practice separatism. We have to be *with* unbelievers, but not *of* them (1 Peter 2:11–12). This is a difficult task because it is much easier to gravitate toward either extreme; it is easier to either separate ourselves to a position of isolation, or to immerse ourselves in the world and thus compromise ourselves and our message. Our behaviors have often culminated in a type of separatism where we are not allowed to associate with the world around us for fear of contamination.

This is taking 2 Corinthians 6:14 out of context where it says, "Do not be yoked together with unbelievers. For what do righteousness and wickedness have in common? Or what fellowship can light have with darkness?" (NIV). In this passage Paul is cautioning us not to engage in a dependent relationship with people who do not embrace the same standards that we do. It will be an unequal relationship; we will suffer for it; we will compromise ourselves because of it.

The original disciples serve as the perfect example of what Hirsch calls "limnality" and how to fellowship with the unbelieving world. Jesus drew them from a contaminated environment, transformed them, and then sent them back from whence they came. We can't be drawn out of that world, be transformed, and then stay out. We have to go back into the world to minister to those who need the gospel most.

As we have done before, we use a secular example to illustrate a spiritual concept by the contrast it offers. If we want to know what fellowship looks like we might watch the History Channel or Discovery Channel when they air documentaries on gang culture in the United States. No, we didn't misspeak—gang culture. Watch them. It doesn't matter if they're Asian, African, Hispanic, or Aryan Brotherhood. They all demonstrate a measure of loyalty, support, and fellowship that should shake Christians to their core.

To be sure, gang fellowship is not Christian fellowship. Gang fellowship has its roots in crime and material gain whereas Christian fellowship is rooted in God and ministry one to another. But a gang is a family having common interests, bonds, and goals. They will do almost anything for their family including stealing, maiming, and even killing. They will give their lives for one another because the gang family fills a void which the members couldn't fill elsewhere.

If criminal gangs devote themselves one to another so deeply for purposes of temporal gain, how much more should we do it for purposes of eternal gain? John Donne wrote, "All mankind is of one author," and, "No man is an island entire unto himself." These words express something we all know at the most basic level—we all have the same origin and are dependent on one another. All people and people groups must have fellowship; we cannot live without it; we will wither without it; we will die without it. There will be no healthy transformation without fellowship, for it is from fellowship that we draw strength from one another.

If we don't have fellowship with future disciples, those yet outside the Body, how will we reach them? Let's face it—the world is an ugly place. If we could avoid being part of it, we would. But we can't avoid it—nor should we try. We are called to be salt and light to this world (Matthew 5:13, 14; Romans 2:19; Acts 26:23). Without going to the unredeemed, how can we impact them for God (Mark 2:15–17)? We must value the, as yet, unredeemed as did Jesus (Luke 9:51–55). Most of all, we must cherish the children who have little chance without seeing God's love for them through us who know the truth (Matthew 19:13–15). It is impossible to proliferate our DNA to others without having fellowship with those yet outside the Body. *do God is Uip! Lead*

How we ## Service and Compassion *w/care!*

To understand what service and compassion are, and why we should give and show them, we should start with 1 Corinthians 13:1, where Paul says, "If I speak in the tongues of men and of angels, but have not love, I am a noisy gong or a clanging cymbal" (ESV). Paul says that if we want to call ourselves Christians, there must be some outward impact on other people's lives—we must give service and compassion to those around us as an earthly example of what God in heaven has done for us. As believers we must understand that our relationship with Him must take a practical form. It's a shopworn phrase, but a meaningful one, to say that love is an action verb. We cannot be complete as believers unless we serve someone in love. True, service is a spiritual gift (1 Corinthians 12:5), but that just means some are specifically so gifted. This doesn't negate the fact that all of us are commanded to serve. If one doesn't have the spiritual gift of service, it doesn't mean that we can ignore that element of our spiritual DNA (Ephesians 2:10).

If we want to make an impact on other people's lives we have at least three choices of how we can relate to them. First, we can give them direction. Second, we can toil alongside them where they are working. Third, we can provide what they need to complete their work.

The first choice is not service—it is a form of leadership. To give direction from a leadership perspective requires a clearly defined and understood relationship between those leading and those being led. Leadership is important: but sometimes we are merely bossy and pass this off as service. And do not be confused because effective leadership is *always* a discipline in service to those persons being led.

The other two choices are forms of hands-on service and can be applied in as many ways as there are situations and people. There are too many service opportunities to list. Here are a few that enjoy marquis billing in today's contemporary culture.

- Benevolent funding for those in financial distress
- Divorce counseling
- Teen pregnancy and abortion counseling
- Gay and lesbian counseling
- Providing for the homeless
- Visitation to the elderly

Every person in need but not ministered to is an indictment against us putting our faith into action. The Bible is clear that the church has the resources, and thus the responsibility, to help. The Old Testament Prophets are steeped in our need to minister to the less fortunate (see also 1 Corinthians 16 and 2 Corinthians 8–9). Some churches are very good at serving, and some are not. The evangelical side of the house isn't holding up its end very well. Why is that? Possibly it's because too many of our resources go toward preaching and teaching—important things to be sure but not the only things. Possibly it's because we fear being accused of practicing a "social gospel." There's nothing wrong with a social gospel as long as it is equally balanced with the gospel of salvation by faith in God's grace alone. Most churches have at least a token community outreach ministry. But if the world we are ministering to is outside the walls of the church, should this not be a *primary* activity? After all, world evangelism is a major biblical thrust (Matthew 28; Acts 1:8). And part of evangelism necessarily includes ministering to real needs so that people are willing and able to hear the truth of Christ. Often we need to first show the compassion of Christ before people are ready to hear about the saving eternal power of Christ.

Too many evangelicals have historically turned a blind eye to poverty and need because it is the easy thing to do. If we pan the landscape things look pretty placid. But, go out onto the spiritual battlefield. The blood and gore flows all around us and those who are bleeding and dying are crying out for someone to help them. It's there—we must look for it. We must serve to be whole Christians. The model for our service should be the sacrifice of Jesus Christ Himself. He served our most basic need by giving up everything He had. Service is part of our spiritual DNA—precisely service to the "least of these" (Matthew 25:40). Service and compassion are different from evangelism and missions. Service and compassion are elements of Christian love applied in a practical way by helping people meet their needs. To be sure, service and compassion often open the doors for evangelism and missions, but the two categories are not fully equivalent. Service and compassion means rolling up our sleeves and helping a world in need; evangelism and missions are preaching and teaching the gospel to those who have not yet heard it (Matthew 28:18–20; Acts 1:8).

Evangelism and Missions

If Christ is our model, and God's plan is for us to be like Him, then Jesus' initial act should be our primary focus. Jesus' initial act was to come into the world. For transformation to occur, the believer must behave like Christ even when he or she would rather do anything but. We spend little time discussing how truly repulsive it must have been for Christ to come into the world. We rightfully focus on His love, patience, and kindness—all of which are legitimate and germane to our lives. But did Jesus have no feelings? If we're created in God's image, and we have feelings, and Jesus is fully human, as well as fully God, than we had better believe that Jesus had feelings. How do we suppose He felt looking down at the fetid mess that we've created for ourselves? Do we suppose He relished the idea of being immersed in this catastrophe we call life—if even for a scant thirty-three years?

The Bible doesn't say much about that aspect of the incarnation, but we can draw some probable conclusions from what we know of God's nature. To understate the obvious, it must have been misery to leave Heaven and be born into the cesspool of humanity. Jesus didn't have to, but He chose to do this out of obedience to the Father (Philippians 2) and out of love for us (John 3:16). Of His own volition, He suffered for a time in this world so that we wouldn't have to suffer for eternity. Not only did He willfully live here for thirty-three years, He was falsely accused, mocked by those over whom He had authority, tried by a kangaroo court, executed in a most barbaric way, and spent three days in the grave wholly separated from His Father. What He did goes far beyond what we traditionally think of when we talk about evangelism and missions. The words, *into the world* and the Great Commission of Matthew 28:18-20, don't begin to describe the enormity of what Christ experienced when He chose to leave Heaven and the right hand of His loving Father.

Take a look at the following references to get a better picture of what going "into the world" means: Psalm 19:4; John 1:9; 3:17; 3:19; 6:14; 9:39; 10:36; 11:27; 12:46; 17:18; 18:37; Romans 10:18; 1 Timothy 1:15; Hebrews 1:6; 10:5; and 1 John 4:9.

Going into the world means going where we would never choose to go—into places that are uncomfortable, disgusting, and frightening. There are teaching and practical missions to the disenfranchised and displaced—some of which are entire nations. There are short-term missions to provide something practical for people who have little. There are inner-city missions to the homeless and other cast-offs of society. There are missions to splinter groups of our culture, many of which would never cross the path of an evangelical Christian if that Christian were to avoid their domain. Some of these are the gay and lesbian communities, prostitutes, people in prison, drug addicts, gamblers, alcoholics, and sexual predators—some worse than this. Did not Jesus model this? After all, He had the reputation of being a friend of sinners (Matthew 11:19). And do we not read in Luke 6:40, "A disciple is not above his teacher, but everyone when he is fully trained will be like his teacher" (ESV)? If Jesus ministered to undesirables, so must we. When Jesus said, "Go into all the world," He didn't mumble. Going into all the world should be the cornerstone of mature spiritual DNA.

How many of us are willing to publicly display the indelible mark of Jesus on our hearts to the young man sitting at the table adjacent to mine as I write this—he who has the pentacle tattooed on his forehead? He knows in whom he has placed his trust or he wouldn't have disfigured his body thusly. How many of us are willing to exercise our spiritual DNA and engage him in a loving conversation while he heaps hatred and filth on that in which we have placed *our* trust? You answer this question in your own heart of hearts—I am ashamed to say that I already have.

These then are what we believe to be the elements of spiritual DNA that are common to all disciples of all times. It is these elements that Our Father intends to develop in each of His children that we might become like Jesus Christ and minister to the real world in which we live.

PARKVIEW BAPTIST CHURCH—Newport News, VA
Spiritual Lean in Action

The Friday evening ministry at Parkview is designated as a time for worship. It's an hour-long service focused on music and prayer, with a fifteen-minute micro-message packing a punch that few if any hour-long traditional sermons can touch. This ministry is fluid, fueled by the experience and emotion of the congregation. In short, it is our Lean ministry. To set it up, we defined value as worship and praise to God, and then we mapped a future value stream showing what we wanted for worship and praise. We made it flow by using prayer and music as our foundation for worship and praise. We respond to pull of both the churched and the unchurched by responding to their needs during the service, and we seek perfection through prayer, praise, and worship.

We have applied Lean to our outreach food ministry as well. By designing this ministry using Lean principles, we allow our community to pull value by meeting a practical need in their lives. We do this without maintaining any work-in-process or standing inventory. We do it without cost to the church and without outside aid. How? We collected data by researching services already existing within the community. We identified that if we could provide food on just one day per month and asked our congregation to bring in very specific items during the two weeks prior to the delivery date, we would need little storage space and could use a small section of our fellowship hall to prepare the bags as they arrived from the members. By not seeking federal and state aid, we cut out the layers of bureaucracy and time spent filling out forms requiring demographics, income, etc. We only ask for a name, address, and family size. We provide this ministry on one Friday each month and we invite the recipients regardless of their circumstances to the Friday evening service.

Both of these ministries are still in their infancy, but already the food ministry has led to three families attending the church regularly and one family finding salvation in Jesus Christ. The Friday evening service continues to grow at a rapid rate and is bringing people in the doors for our Sunday contemporary and traditional services.

The ironic thing is when the subject of applying proven business tools (Lean, Theory of Constraints, and Six Sigma) to the church was initially broached, there were some who thought I was the anti-Christ, some who were extremely hesitant, and some who were enthusiastic. By carefully sowing seeds, being persistent, and providing sound data, though adapted from the business world, we have started on our Lean ministry and changed the minds of most. Our biggest obstacle was convincing the church that we are not perverting the fundamentals in which we believe, we are not becoming worldly at the expense of God's principle, but are instead repackaging God's Message in its entirety in a modern form of worship with less waste than is typically found in the traditional church.

– Rusty Beck, Senior Pastor
Randy Braddock, Lean Sigma Black Belt

Chapter 6

The Seven Deadly Wastes

"When I think back on all the crap I learned in high school
It's a wonder I can think at all.
And though my lack of education
Hasn't hurt me none
I can read the writing on the wall."

–Paul Simon, 1973
"Kodachrome"

If Lean defines and provides opportunities to eliminate waste, and we intend to use it in the transformation process, we must have an understanding of where waste occurs in ministry. This chapter defines that waste, gives some examples, and lays the foundation for eliminating such waste from your ministry.

We have established that value is produced when something is transformed from one state into another, and that waste is anything we do or anything we have that does not contribute directly to value. In the case of ministry, waste is anything we do or anything we have that does not contribute directly to the transformation of our spiritual DNA—note that we used the word *directly*. If you're honest, we think you will agree that the church universal generates quite a bit of waste.

Before you get discouraged, let's break it down a little by using the example of the hydraulic cylinder cited earlier in the book. Cutting, milling, and polishing a piece of steel into a component that will be of use to the customer are all activities that add value. What does not add value is all the time that component waits to be processed or travels around the factory; no value is produced when we make it wrong and have to start over again; no value is added when we put it in inventory because we will probably use it someday…but not today. Also, when it's in inventory we have to count it, move it, and handle it. Sometimes, when we handle it, we damage it and have to repair or scrap it. That takes time and effort and costs money. No value is produced for the customer when we make more of anything than the customer can actually use when it's completed.

Those are non-value-added activities that are relatively easy to recognize. But there are some that are not so easy to see. For example, there was an engineering department in that factory whose engineers designed that product. But those engineers did not add value because they did not transform something from one state into another. The factory needs a sophisticated database with which to track their costs and the expenditure of their resources. But while the database and computing equipment are necessary, they do not transform anything so they do not add value. Each department in that factory has a manager who adds no value. The factory is housed in a building so the workers can be warm in the winter and cool in the summer. But the building and the energy it consumes add no value.

These are some examples of value-added and non-value-added activities with which most of us can identify and easily understand. But many of them are necessary; we will not be able to eliminate them all. We need engineers to design the product. We need databases to track our costs and resources. We need leadership in each of the areas of the factory. We need a building for our people to work in. But, as a starting point Lean classifies any activity or anything we have or use as either value or waste.

Value Stream Mapping

Value stream mapping is a Lean technique used to define all the value-added and non-value-added steps in the production of any good or service. We won't go into great detail here; suffice it to say that the value stream map produces a numerical answer, giving the ratio of value to waste in any process. A world-class Lean organization cannot eliminate much more than about 25% of its waste. This means, if we begin with 100% and whittle down the waste, only 25% of a world-class organization's total expended effort goes toward providing value to the customer; the other 75%, although non-value-adding, is tolerated as necessary to the operation.

Organizations not using Lean have much more than 25% waste. Sometimes the waste approaches 95% or more. Strangely, many organizations actually make a profit having only 3–5% of their total expended effort providing value. Please know that this is not our opinion—these are measurable facts.

Any waste has a round-robin, or domino type, effect on every other waste. Each waste contributes to all others resulting in a dynamic effect that exponentially degrades the effectiveness of the entire system.

To broadly categorize our resources, we can say that any activity, or thing, or person, in any organization, including a church, can be classified as one of three types.

Type 1:	That which provides true value for our customer by directly transforming something from one state into another.
Type 2:	That which provides no value but is unavoidable due to some legitimate constraint or requirement in how we operate.
Type 3:	That which provides no value and is immediately avoidable. These are the most damaging and are the primary focus of Lean implementation.

Figure 6.1: Three Types of Resources

The church has all three types of activities just like any other organization. Types 1 and 2 should be easy to identify. Type 1 provides value and many Type 2 activities cannot be eliminated for good reasons. Organizations in the secular world that implement Lean very realistically understand that they cannot eliminate all forms of waste. Some waste must be tolerated for us to make the product and get it out the door. But how much waste can we tolerate and how do we know which is which? Also there are gray areas within Type 2 that should be examined because sometimes we uncritically continue to do things just because we've always done it that way. Only by value stream mapping the transformation processes of a particular church would we know that answer.

It is the Type 3 activities in the church that we must target first—those activities that add no value and can be stopped immediately.

Defining Waste

To do this we must define waste in terms that we can all understand. Waste was broadly categorized by Shigeo Shingo, a Toyota engineer, into seven common elements. He said, "Waste is waste, whether you're making automobiles or baking bread." We might add here, "…or making disciples."

Overproduction:	Producing more than what is necessary at the moment; making or acquiring anything that isn't needed; producing product sooner than is required; waiting for large batches to be processed all at the same time. Overproduction contributes to the other six forms of waste
Correction:	Production of defective products causing us to repair or scrap them and make them all over again.
Inventory:	Inventory of any type that is more than what we immediately need to satisfy our customer's desires
Waiting:	Waiting for anything, such as: workers waiting for parts; machines waiting for work-in-process; people waiting for information; good parts waiting for reworked parts to be completed.
Motion:	Excess or unnecessary human, manufactured parts, or machine motion. Some is necessary, but must be minimized.
Movement:	Moving people, material or information from one place to another. Some is necessary, but must be minimized.
Overprocessing:	Any processing that neither improves the quality of the product, nor is required by the customer.

Figure 6.2: Secular Lean's Definitions of Waste

Overproduction:	Teaching or preaching to large batches of disciples at the same time has potential to be a terrible waste because all are not in need of the same message, nor are all at the same place on the timeline of the transformation process.
Correction:	Defective theology or theology taken out of context and used as a foundation for self-serving purposes. This takes a lifetime to correct.
Inventory:	All the members of the congregation who are hearers only and not involved in a practical way in the transformation process (James 1:22); the inventory of spiritual gifts resident in the congregation, many of which are never applied to the transformation process (Romans 12; 1 Corinthians 12, 14; 1 Peter 4); financial resources tied up in unnecessarily elaborate buildings and grounds having no positive impact on the transformation process.
Waiting:	Missionaries ready and willing to serve but waiting for funding because it takes, on average, almost 3 years of deputation before reaching the field; disciples in the congregation having distinct spiritual gifts waiting for the church to apply them to the transformation process; disciples in a large batch waiting vainly for a sermon relative to their place on the transformation timeline and applicable to their particular needs today.

Motion:	People activities associated with programs and processes having little or nothing to do with the transformation processes of the people-group at hand. Ministries that are focused more on interests and hobbies rather than making true disciples of Christ.
Movement:	The movement of people in and through church programs having little or nothing to do with the transformation process of the people group at hand.
Overprocessing:	Separating the congregation into batches by age or gender and placing them in classes or groups with the assumption that God transforms people by demographic; hearing introductory-level sermons over and over; music, instruments, worship teams, choirs, and other productions having more entertainment value than impact on the transformation process.

Figure 6.3: Lean Ministry's Definitions of Waste

We have extrapolated the seven categories of waste originally defined by Mr. Shingo to apply to the church and give some examples of activities or things not contributing directly to the transformation process.

Thus far, most of you have probably had no significant disagreement with Lean ministry theory. It is now when interesting discussions may arise. A number of you may mount the argument that goes something like this, "But we're different. We're not a business. We're on a loftier spiritual plane and not constrained by these baser principles. Besides, we have the Holy Spirit to guide us."

All of this is true, and forgive us for being blunt, but please spare us this wasteful objection. Applying Lean principles to ministry is new, but we have heard this self-serving argument more times than we can count in the thirty-plus years we have been in the change implementation business. If we mount this argument it is nothing more than an attempt to demonstrate some measure of superficial control over our own circumstances—whether it makes any sense or not. Your situation is not different. All ministries have value-added activities and wasteful activities—period. It's up to all of us to figure out the difference between the two and understand and apply what will work best in the venue where God has placed us.

Back to our discussion—the seven categories of waste listed above define our target. Targeting wasteful activities for elimination is analogous to golf. What does the golfer do when he gets into the T-box and addresses the ball? What does he hope to accomplish? Does he intend to move the ball closer to the cup by hitting a series of strokes that move forward in 45-degree angles—much like a sailboat tacks into the wind? Does a golfer hit it in the general direction and simply hope for the best? Or does he take careful aim, balance his stance, discipline his body, and try to hit a hole-in-one with each stroke? Of course, he tries to hit the hole-in-one. How many times does that happen in a golfer's lifetime? Seldom, if ever. But, excellence is defined by understanding the nature of our target, understanding the nature of the elements preventing us from reaching our target, and systematically reducing errors and wasteful efforts until we've achieved our end result. Then the savvy competitor goes back to square one and begins the process all over again until the next end result is better than the last.

Don't conclude that we must hit a hole-in-one every time we swing the club. What we should do is open our minds and consider the nature of our targets and the sequence of events that will move us in that direction most expeditiously.

Eliminating the waste in our ministries is challenging enough without adding something Lean calls a *counterbalance*. A counterbalance is something that we cannot compromise in the name of improvement. We cannot stress strongly enough how important the counterbalance is in Lean ministry. The counterbalances to improvements generated through Lean in ministry are the essence of what God the Father considers valuable; the integrity of the individual disciple; and the elements of what makes a disciple. Our challenge lies in the elimination of waste while keeping our counterbalance intact. We must not compromise what we are doing with the way we do it.

We're all hyper-conditioned to look for waste in a business environment, or in sporting events, or in our personal cash flow, or in any other activity that produces a definable and easy-to-measure impact on our personal lives. When we recognize a loss we rush to make a correction because we are losing our precious personal resources.

But it takes an open mind, unencumbered by tradition and personal biases, to see waste where our efforts produce something intangible, as in the development of disciples. All seven wastes are resident in the most important area of our lives and that which we should take most personally—our spiritual life and our church. If the transformation of the disciple is valued most highly by God, we must relentlessly seek out waste. We must be contributors of value and destroyers of waste to support God's intent to transform mankind.

Value and waste are mutually exclusive in any organization. The acceptance of wasteful behaviors, and the wasteful use of what God has given us, financial or otherwise, degrades the ability of the church to fulfill its mission. It minimizes the efficacy of those persons within a given church who are focused on making an impact on lives and are trying to lead the transformation process.

This passive tolerance, and sometimes active encouragement of efforts not contributing directly to the development of the individual disciple, amounts to spiritual malfeasance of the first water. We believe this is equivalent to Jesus' words to the church of Sardis recorded in Revelation 3:1–3, where He says, "I know your works. You have the reputation of being alive, but you are dead. Wake up, and strengthen what remains and is about to die, for I have not found your works complete in the sight of my God. Remember, then, what you received and heard. Keep it, and repent. If you will not wake up, I will come like a thief, and you will not know at what hour I will come against you" (ESV).

Not all organizations harbor all seven forms of waste at equal levels of severity. The type of process, the organization's culture, and the venue in which the organization finds itself determine the relative damage done by each type of waste. We feel that the most damaging wastes in Christian ministry are overproduction, inventory, and correction.

The following is a closer look at the seven categories of waste and how they damage our mission.

Overproduction and Batch Processing

Lean sees overproduction as the root of all manufacturing evil because, even though it is a waste itself, it contributes to the other six forms of waste. The principal cause of overproduction is batch processing. Batch processing means we do the same thing to a large batch of individual pieces, parts, or people—all at the same time. At face value, this sounds good—it sounds efficient. But upon closer examination we see some problems. It assumes that the entire batch is in need of the same process at the same time. Most often they're not. Also, the first item processed doesn't go anywhere until the last item in the batch receives the same treatment. All the pieces, parts, or people wait for everything or everyone behind them to catch up to wherever they are, so the batch can only move as quickly as the slowest part. Each of the items are treated the same and are forced to wait for each other when they should each be moving toward some next value-adding step. Batch processing and overproducing are for the convenience of the processor and not for the convenience of either the product or the customer. Just because we have the capacity to process large batches of people doesn't mean that we should or that it makes sense.

We do a lot of overproduction in the traditional evangelical church, and we do it by batch processing. In fact, the twenty-first-century church is masterful at batch processing. How we conduct the Sunday morning service is a good example. The traditional twenty-first-century church calls what happens on Sunday morning a "worship service." But the typical Sunday morning service consists of about fifteen minutes of announcements, another fifteen minutes of singing, and a short sermon. We call this worship, but there is very little worshiping done in many Sunday morning services. What really happens is some teaching and housekeeping with a seasoning of music. Because the Sunday service is the centerpiece of the church, this practice of batch processing is exported to many, if not most, of the other programs.

In *The Forgotten Ways*, Alan Hirsch says the primary activities of the church have been reduced to preaching and teaching, both occurring mostly inside the church building. If he's correct, we must make sure that we're doing those two things as best we can. There is nothing wrong with teaching. Jesus was a teacher—Jesus was *the* teacher. Most of what Jesus did was teaching. So, if He is our teaching model, we should make sure that our teaching and preaching methods are actually an effective transfer of information from the people who know something to the people who need to learn something.

Any learning journey must have a starting point. To successfully learn anything we need to get a firm grasp on the underlying principles, the models, and the basic methodologies of our subject. We need to establish a foundation. Consider this a general information dump to the unlearned—a good example is how many of us started out our higher education experience.

Go back a few years. Those of you who took English 101 at a large land-grant university in the '70s will remember the huge class sizes of 500–700 students with the lecture delivered via closed-circuit TV. Or think about how Introduction to College Algebra was delivered in a monotone by a lecturer whose first language was not English. In the case of closed-circuit TV, the student could not participate; the student could not ask questions; the student could not give feedback and get clarification. In the case of the ESL instructor, trying to interact was just too much trouble. After all, mathematics is its own language, isn't it? It's a wonder that any of us graduated.

Even so, having one person lecture to a large group to provide the beginning information dump and kick off English 101 or College Algebra was, and still is, the most effective and efficient way to establish a baseline for continued learning for large groups of students—all of whom are at about the same place in their journey of academic transformation. This one-way transfer of information is what happens on Sunday morning in many churches.

We question the efficiency and effectiveness of this learning procedure as the only or best method. When a lecturer stands before a group of students or a preacher before a congregation there are assumptions in play that may or may not be true. The first assumption is that he knows something that they don't know, and also that they should know it. The second assumption is that the congregation has nothing to contribute to the lecturer, demonstrated by the fact that there is no opportunity for them to make a contribution. The third assumption is that each member of the congregation has nothing of value to contribute to the other members of the congregation—again, there is no opportunity to do so. The fourth assumption is that all members of the congregation are in need of the same message at this time.

The first assumption is most likely true but the other three are false. It is true that many preachers know more about their subject than do most members of their congregation. They have something to teach and the congregation has something to learn. It is not true that the congregation has nothing to contribute to the preacher. Most, if not all, of them have practical problems and oftentimes practical and theologically correct solutions to their problems that the preacher is never exposed to. It is also not true that any given member of the congregation has nothing to contribute to the other members—everyone has something from which everyone else can learn. Finally, it is not true that all members of the congregation are in need of the same message at this time. All are in unique places along the transformation process.

Some pastors regularly seek feedback from a variety of listeners by using a small, diversified, rotating group of laymen and laywomen who are asked to contribute to a discussion on illustrations, applications, and insights on future passages to be taught. Such insights can be invaluable to the pastor as he prepares his message. We wish more pastors did this.

Without feedback, one-way transfers of information are just as counterproductive for the speaker as they are for the listener. The speaker cannot make real-time adjustments to the message, or refocus what is being taught, to better communicate the subject. If the speaker waits until next week, the message is too far in the past and he must take precious time to correct what he said a week ago. A one-way transfer of information concludes that the speaker assumes everyone has the same ability to assimilate the same information and that everyone is at the same place on God's *takt* timeline.

No doubt this worked very well a number of centuries ago. It probably worked very well until the mid-fifteenth century when Gutenberg published the first Bible. At that time, preaching to large groups made sense—in fact, the larger the group the better. But the world began to change with Gutenberg. Today we have not only high literacy rates, but the Internet gives us limitless access to information. The Butterfly Effect has come into its own in the world of information transfer.

Lest you think we have gone off the track, let us say it again: It is true that we all have something to learn by passively listening to one person speak. But is this the best method? Should we put all our eggs in this one basket? How much is really learned through batch teaching? How well does it work in our present world?

Within the twenty-first-century church there is a wide range of biblical literacy. Brand-new converts who have only been exposed to a few passages of Scripture cannot be expected to hang in there with believers who have been walking with the Lord and studying His Word for several decades. No first-rate university would dream of a one-size-fits-all, batch-processing learning methodology for all their students regardless of their level of development. They would go out of business in a heartbeat. The higher you go in the secular learning food chain the smaller the class sizes get. People don't learn well in batches unless they are learning the most basic subject matter. Higher-level learning takes place in small groups.

In the church we don't do a very good job of harnessing group learning dynamics to facilitate a supercharged transfer of information. In the Sunday service there is one learning dynamic in play. That dynamic is the transfer of information from the speaker to the listeners, no matter how many of them there are or where they are in the transformation process. Information travels in one direction with few, if any, course corrections along the way.

Learning dynamics increase exponentially as the group size increases and then begin to deteriorate rapidly after the group reaches a certain size. Consider two small groups of people learning from each other: One is a group of two persons and one is a group of three persons. In the first group there are two learning dynamics. Person A learns from Person B and Person B learns from Person A. In the second group there are six learning dynamics. Person A learns from Persons B and C. Person B learns from Persons A and C. And Person C learns from Persons A and B.

The table below shows the theoretical learning dynamics within different group sizes. In a group of four persons there are twelve learning dynamics. In a group of five persons there are twenty learning dynamics. In a group of six there are thirty learning dynamics…and so on.

At some point the number of potential learning dynamics becomes unmanageable. Figure 5.4 shows that it can go to an absurd length—a congregation of 200 people would have 200 X 199 = 39,800 learning dynamics. In truth, groups become unmanageable at a much smaller size. From experience, the point of unmanageability is somewhere around 12 persons. It is interesting to observe that group dynamics become unmanageable at about the same number as were the original disciples.

Group Size	Theoretical Learning Dynamics
1	1
2	2
3	6
4	12
5	20
6	30
7	42
8	56
9	72
10	90
11	110
12	132
13	156
14	182
15	210
16	240
17	272
18	306
19	342
20	380
...	...
200	39,800

Figure 6.4: Learning Dynamics by Group Size

Many churches encourage and facilitate small groups, but they are usually not the primary focus of the church's activities. The smaller the group the better the learning. The most effective learning, development, and transformation take place one-on-one. Lean strives for one-piece flow in any process. But in the real world, one-on-one is just as unreasonable as one-on-two hundred. So, if one-on-one isn't possible, and one-on-two hundred is unmanageable, we need to reduce the batch size to something that is both manageable and effective.

Correction

Whereas we talked about overproduction at a corporate level in the church, we see correction making its impact at an individual level. In the context of this book we define correction as defective theology or theology taken out of context and used as a foundation for self-serving purposes. Some people grow up in churches where Christianity and the Bible were completely misrepresented. This can take years to undo even after these folks find a solid church with effective ministry. On an individual level this is the most damaging of all forms of waste. In manufacturing, making a defect results in one of two things. We either rework it into a suitable product or we scrap it. If we rework it, the cost is roughly 300% of what it should have been, because rework actually results in doing the same job three times. First, we make it wrong. Second, we undo the error. Third, we rework it into something that the customer can use. If we decide to scrap a defective part, we have to make another one to replace it. When we consider rescheduling and all the double and triple handling involved, the cost to make something wrong and discard it skyrockets to 350%.

Reworking defective theology is very difficult and time consuming. And we can't throw the disciple away simply because they use defective theology. We are all familiar with the old argument about how many angels can dance on the head of a pin. It is an analogy describing a type of meaningless controversy that generates nonproductive discussions about things that either cannot be proven or do not contribute to God's mission in any way. Yet we continue to engage in the same type of meaningless discussions about unimportant attributes of both church and individual behaviors. It seems incredible, but we still hear sermons preached on what is the most correct translation of the Bible. Have we forgotten that what we call the Bible came from many manuscripts and that the original texts were not written in English? Simply translating the original texts into English loses part of the original meaning. Add to this dress codes, types of music, and many other opportunities for disagreement, and we introduce a great deal of waste in the form of defective or wide-of-the-mark theology.

If we make a defect in a disciple, be it willful or otherwise, we cause damage that takes years, if not an entire lifetime, to correct. Sadly, sometimes it is never corrected. Jesus has strong words for teachers who peddle defective theology or useless debates (James 3:1-6; Colossians 2:16–23). Many of us are living examples of this type of waste. For some of us who have been believers since we were toddlers, the ensuing 30, 40 or 50+ years our theology and understanding of God have been jaded by an eclectic and unrelated mix of divisive positions on the following:

- Amillenial position
- Pre-millenial position
- Covenantalist
- Arminian
- Sovereignty
- Baptist
- Anabaptist
- Conditional security
- Casual dress codes
- Dispensationalist
- Calvinism
- Free will
- King James Only
- Lutheranism
- Presbyterianism
- Eternal Security
- Acceptable dress codes

Like Paul Simon says, "It's a wonder I can think at all." We would like to say that what unites us is much greater than what divides us, but, sadly, that is not true across the board.

We all have convictions on many of the issues listed. But for years, many believers lead spiritually stunted lives because of the conflicts between splinter theologies within the same church body. We may not rationalize them clearly in our minds, but we end up living our lives as impotent Christians because our pathway is obscured by the waste of this conflict.

While some of the issues listed above are theologically important, many of them are not. Many of the issues that the church debates are embarrassing and counterproductive to transformation. We could pick some low-hanging fruit: snake handling, selling indulgences, and debates over the color of the carpet. How we go about debating some of the more important things are equally as silly: alcohol or no alcohol; tobacco or no tobacco; dancing or no dancing; piano vs. organs vs. guitars and drums. Dare we have Celebrate Recovery, Divorce Care, or AA meetings in our church lest we appear liberal? We have divisions over questionable and unknowable end-times issues and to have or not have a cross in the front of the sanctuary—and whether that cross must be empty. We argue about cathedral or modern type buildings. We engage in endless hair splitting on minimally important theological issues in which sincere believers come to different conclusions and often generate hard feelings.

Many Christians and churches endure this nonsense which destroys unity and retards transformation. It is a terrible thing that many of us have embraced these peripheral issues as central to our faith. Such damage is not slight. Biblical principles, centered on the gospel, are not hard to understand unless we arrogantly seek to complicate them to demonstrate how much more we know about them than the other people—whoever the other people are. It's time to start afresh with the basics of what we are doing and why we are doing it.

Inventory

Inventory is storing anything that we are not presently using or anything that our customer cannot use. Inventory represents consumption of our resources without immediate purpose. Inventory is the result of overproduction and exacerbates any other waste we already have; inventory never makes a positive contribution. Compiling more than what we need at the moment impedes all other value-added activities by consuming resources that could be applied more constructively elsewhere. If there was a good reason for us to produce it, it would already have been used. We certainly may need it at some time in the future—but then again we may not. In any case, we don't need it right now. If we did, it wouldn't be inventory.

Inventory is the greatest visual indicator that an organization is not lean. Organizations that maintain inventories, or encourage building inventory as an acceptable behavior, demonstrate that the processes are not flowing and valuable resources have been applied to non-value-added activities.

Many, if not most, evangelical churches are heavily burdened with inventory. It's not quite as readily identifiable as seeing large work-in-process inventories on the factory floor, but it's there in a big way. We don't see it because we haven't learned to see it. Two of the most wasteful inventories in the church today are represented by lost human potential and misused dollars.

Human Potential Inventory. The loss of human potential is so devastating that, when implementing Lean, some organizations add it as an eighth category of waste. This is a legitimate addition but was omitted by Mr. Shingo because it should be self-evident that all seven forms of waste contribute directly to the loss of our greatest resource—people. In ministry, it is our people, the individual disciples, who are all-important. They suffer the greatest counterproductive impact if we don't control that which degrades their development and their deployment.

In any given church we have large inventories of people who are hearers only (James 1:22) and not involved in a practical way in any ministry. But the Bible is clear that upon acceptance of Christ, each believer is given at least one spiritual gift for the purpose of glorifying God (1 Peter 4:11) and building up the local church (1 Corinthians 12:7-11). Many of these gifts are never applied to the transformation process even though our customer, God, has an immediate desire to use them for His Glory. There are at least two reasons for this unusable inventory. First, it is possible that the individual doesn't care to use his or her spiritual gift. Second, it is possible that the church has not provided a clear opportunity to assess the individual's spiritual gifts or communicated a clear need for deployment. If spiritual gifts are not being used, it is, at least in part, incumbent upon the church to accept this responsibility.

The loss of disciple potential is devastating to our mission. In ground-level terms, the loss of disciple effectiveness is a loss of weaponry to support the battle in which we are all engaged (Ephesians 6:12). Christian churches the world over contain untold inventories of weapons of mass destruction, embodied in gifted believers, that dwarf today's world military powers. These are gifts of the Spirit and the power of God's Spirit is incalculable when compared to even the most powerful earthly weapons. Unless we have an understanding of those God-empowered WMDs, and a simple waste-free plan for their deployment, we will never get them to the battlefield.

And, by the way, where is the battlefield? Many churches behave as if the battle is inside the church. We have been behaving this way for a long time. Read 1 and 2 Corinthians where Paul talks about a congregation constantly warring against itself. There are legitimate spiritual battles going on inside the church, such as described in Galatians, but the main battle is raging on the outside (Ephesians 6:10–18). This is where our main weaponry should be deployed. Make no mistake about it—every sanctified believer is a Holy Spirit–empowered weapon (Acts 1:8). There are no neutral participants; you must pick a side and fight on it. As Harvey Cox, one of the preeminent initiators of the postmodern ethos, said, "Not to decide is to decide."

Even though every Christian is a weapon, not everyone is a warfighter or a leader of spiritual warfighters. In all battles there are warfighters and there are those who support warfighters. Which one are you? It is hard to tell which one you are unless someone has helped you understand it with a spiritual gifts assessment. It is harder still to be deployed against the enemy if the transformation process does not provide you a role in which to be deployed. If we do not clearly understand God's values, the mission of the church, the transformation process, and the unique venue in which the transformation process takes place, we are just another smart bomb sitting on the shelf waiting for the battle to come to us.

Financial Inventory. Financial resources tied up in buildings and grounds are a Type 2 waste, meaning they do not add value because they have no direct impact on the transformation process but are necessary to get the job done. They have an indirect impact because we need buildings, grounds, music systems, chairs, and classrooms. But these items only permit the transformation process—they do not cause the transformation process. It is all too easy to go overboard and tie up our limited financial resources in elaborate architecture, landscaping, and decorating, while these resources should be better applied at more strategic points. And they may communicate to outsiders that one has to be pretty special to be a part of this group.

By pointing this out we do not advocate some form of self-serving and self-imposed austerity. But we tend to spend considerably more on our buildings, grounds, interiors, and sound systems than is necessary. If we spend more on our facilities than needed, or expand beyond expected reasonable growth, we are wasting one of God's basic resources—His money. Christianity should have a dignified exterior and should be presented as being orderly and in control, but modest. There is no modesty in either the extreme of conspicuous consumption or the extreme of false piety. Both send a strong negative signal to those we would reach for Christ. This is particularly damaging in light of the fact that Christians, as a group, give grudgingly of our finances.

The Barna Group is a California-based Christian information gathering and data analysis group focusing on the information needs of the church. It offers statistics, resources, seminars, and custom research on current cultural and spiritual trends. According to their website, very few born-again Americans tithe. Eighty-three percent of all Americans give some money to one or more non-profit organization and approximately 16% of all born-again Christians give some money to the church. But only about 8% give what the Old Testament refers to as a tithe.

Less than 2% of adults under the age of 40 tithe. These people are our future. After factoring in inflation, and considering the present value of money, churches are actually getting about 2% less than they did in 1999.

Barna says people don't give much for the following five reasons:

1. The church fails to provide a compelling vision for how the money will make a difference in the world.
2. Some see their finances as leverage on the future. They withhold money from the church because they do not see a sufficient return on their investment.
3. Some do not realize the church needs their money in order to be effective.
4. Many are ignorant of what the Bible teaches about our responsibility to apply God's resources in ways that affect lives.
5. There are those who are just selfish. They reason that they worked hard for their money and it's theirs to use as they please.

The church can and should address items 1–4. We can provide and communicate a compelling vision for giving. We can present a return-on-investment for monies given, if not in financial terms. We can respectfully explain that the church needs finances to execute its mission. We can teach our people what the Bible says about giving, using both Old and New Testaments (Malachi 3; 1 Corinthians 16; 2 Corinthians 8–9). There isn't much we can do about people who are selfish; giving up self-centeredness is a hallmark of Christian maturity. God can and will work with selfish people in whatever way He chooses.

Oddly, Barna says the more a person makes the less likely that person is to give, which is especially sad since we live in the wealthiest nation in world history. But it's even sadder when we consider it from the perspective that we are the ones fortunate enough to know the truth about where our money comes from and what should be done with it.

Our giving potential far exceeds our actual behavior. The most recently available U.S. Census Bureau information shows median household income for 2007 as $50,740 and the median size of the American household as 2.56 persons. The gross annual income for a modest-size church of 200 persons and 78 households will average $3,964,063 per year. A tithe of that amount is a very significant $396,406. Barna reports that most churches receive far less than what the Bible considers a reasonable giving potential—that potential being demonstrated by the previous paragraph. Jesus affirms the Old Testament doctrine of tithing in Matthew 23:23, and elsewhere. However, the New Testament emphasizes sacrificial giving—each of us sacrificing for one another based on Christ's perfect example (1 Corinthians 16). Giving cheerfully of our financial wealth is simply one element of that sacrifice (2 Corinthians 8:10–12; 9:7). But should sacrificial giving be less than the Old Testament law commands? Probably not—actually, definitely not! Yet a tithe might be a good place to start.

As we said earlier, we believe that overproduction, correction, and inventory are the most damaging forms of waste extant in the twenty-first-century church. Waiting, motion, movement, and overprocessing also degrade the ability of the church to reach a needy world. But we feel that these last four wastes are largely a result of the first three.

Waiting

There is a lot of waiting done in the typical twenty-first-century evangelical church. Many denominations and churches require their missionaries to raise their own funding before deploying to the field. Even if those missionaries are qualified, willing, and able to fulfill God's call, their departures are delayed one, two, three, or more years while they assemble the necessary funds. Then they must come home every few years and repeat the process of deputation rather than enjoying a well-earned rest.

It is entirely reasonable to ask a willing missionary to demonstrate certain qualifications to perform on the mission field—among them acceptable spirituality, education, health, emotional and spiritual support, cultural awareness, and long-term devotion. It is wasteful to ask a missionary to generate their own support because to do so delays their impact for the Kingdom.

Granted, generating one's own support surely develops a significant level of ownership and ensures a minimum of irresponsible behavior on the part of any given person or family. Yet to delay deputizing candidates from reaching the field, often for several years, is to waste money *and* precious ministry field time. Many potential missionaries fail to get to the field after years of futile deputation while others, who might be inclined to go, choose other careers precisely because of their distaste for this process. All of this constitutes waste which, in turn, begets more waste. The fields are ripe for harvest, and a world vision mandates better use of resources (Matthew 9:37–38).

No for-profit organization, having a clear understanding of its accountability to its stockholders or its customers, would dream of asking a department or an employee of that organization to raise outside support for an improvement initiative. Results-based organizations budget monies for needs they know will arise. The screening process is performed when individual people are placed in leadership positions to execute those improvement initiatives—and they are held accountable for good stewardship.

An example of a successful screening process in use in the church today is the church planter assessment program by Converge Worldwide (CWW). Employment of this structured screening process determines if church planters are able and truly willing to successfully plant a church and have it survive. The prospective church planter is assessed as being in one of three categories: qualified; not qualified; or, potentially qualified if the church planter makes certain changes. This process has increased the five-year survival rate within CWW church plants from approximately 60% to 95% and saved a great deal of CWW funds in the bargain. Could we not budget for at least *known* missions expectations and screen our missionaries to ensure a proper fit to their and our Lord's vision rather than make them wait while they raise their own funding? If we did they would be in the field both faster and cheaper.

Another example of waiting is those members of our congregations having distinct spiritual gifts but who are waiting for the church to apply them. We only have three ways to employ these spiritual gifts. We can direct our members to employ them. We can ignore our member's gifts and hope the Holy Spirit will convict them to employ them. Or we can construct a program and process to identify their spiritual gifts, communicate the need to use their spiritual gifts, and connect the gifted person to a need in the church or community. Options one and two don't work very well and we don't focus as well as we ought on number three. Meanwhile, our people wait.

Motion

Economy of motion is fundamental to Lean because it describes the waste of a resource that we cannot replace—the effort of our people. Motion in a church is a little more difficult to see than some of the other wastes. But if we define motion as people-effort, expended on programs and ministries, it becomes a little easier to grasp. Motion in this case describes a waste of the church staff, be they paid or voluntary. In either case, they are finite and we must use them as such. Their effort, associated with that motion, will be wasted unless our people activities are directly linked to the transformation of our people group.

Each program we have, and every activity we sanction in the church, will consume some staff effort. Many churches expend staff effort to lead programs that are not directly linked to the transformation process. Lean considers these programs wasteful. Ergo, if we have wasteful programs we will be wasting the motions of the people that we ask to lead them. Consider mission trips to other countries to paint churches so the next short-term missions group can come and paint them a different color. If we do an impartial analysis of the local church's programs and measure their effectiveness we may be surprised to learn that some of them have little or no desired effect, or the desired effect was wrong in the first place—wasted motion.

Movement

Movement is a waste that is also more difficult to see in a church, but much more damaging to the church than the waste of motion because it applies to those for whom we are expected to provide the opportunity for transformation—our people group.

We provide opportunities for our people to move into, through, and out of as many programs as there are people to conceive of them. But if we don't directly link each of those programs to transformation, we become unwittingly wasteful. If we continue to maintain programs not contributing directly to the transformation process for either misguided reasons, or because of the discomfort associated with change, people will naturally gravitate toward them and fill them up. Nature abhors a vacuum. Thus we have institutionalized behaviors that we should have avoided in the first place, causing our people a great deal of nonproductive movement. This includes any program not purposefully designed for outreach and discipleship. Social, sports, and casual fellowship programs can be transformational with wise intentional design. But too often they are merely recreational and eat up ministry resources, people resources, staff resources, and time. Such programs must be honestly evaluated for their real contribution to the transformation of disciples.

Overprocessing

Overprocessing things that don't matter much, if at all, is so wasteful as to be deserving of its own category. Some churches unintentionally overprocess people because they haven't thought it through; others do it intentionally because it feels good. Overprocessing in ministry is to treat someone, or a group of people, as if they need something when they really don't. Often we conduct our Christian education by separating the congregation into batches by age or gender and placing them in classes with the assumption that God transforms people by age and gender. Any people group is very much matrixed with regard to their interests, abilities, and strengths and weaknesses—and, of course, their needs. Separating them by age and gender is for the convenience of the processor and not for those processed.

An example of overprocessing is preaching a salvation sermon every Sunday to a congregation, many of whom have been believers since they were very young, based on the possibility that there may be an unbeliever in church that Sunday. True, the unbeliever cannot believe unless they hear the Word (Romans 10:15). But, in these cases, the bulk of the listeners sit patiently listening to something they have heard many times before and have known for a long time and often tune out as a result. It is highly likely that the unbelieving listener would be more impressed with a sermon on the deeper Christian life, demonstrating the existence of an entire belief structure that he or she didn't know existed, than a sermon on conversion from a lifestyle they are comfortable with—because it's the only one they know. It seems that theologically astute, biblically conditioned sermons ought to contain opportunities to share the gospel almost weekly—without making the entire sermon evangelistic to an audience the majority of which have already walked the aisle during fifteen verses of "Just As I Am."

One might also consider the very slickly produced spiritual variety show found in some churches. The "Church of the Really Big Show" badly overprocesses people hungry for transformation with music, instruments, worship teams, choirs, drama teams, movies, and other productions having more entertainment value than the potential to transform lives.

Lastly, we have the ongoing timeless arguments over biblical translations, dress codes, peripheral theological issues, music styles, and other issues too numerous to mention. But the most non-productive and overprocessed subject of all is exactly when Jesus will return (Matthew 24:36).

KENSINGTON CHURCH—Troy, MI
Deming's Plan-Do-Check-Act Cycle

It seems so simple, doesn't it? First, we should make a plan. Second, we should initiate the plan. Next, we should check our progress as to how well the plan is going. Finally, we should take what we learned from checking the plan to make some adjustments and get the job done better, on time, and without wasting our precious resources. If it's so simple, why don't we do it more often? Perhaps we think it's so simple we don't have to do it.

Kensington Church of Troy, Michigan, recently executed a simple serving project using Dr. Edwards Deming's Plan-Do-Check-Act cycle—a key practice in Lean. For those of you not familiar with Dr. Deming, he is largely credited with leading the reconstruction of Japan's economy after World War II. He did it using simple principles, which Kensington Church is trying to emulate.

While our campus was still in the planning stages but our presence in the community had already been announced, we decided to do a serving project. The campus leaders planned it and set it in motion. We were to renovate a house in Pontiac, Michigan, and build a barrier-free ramp so a special-needs eighteen-year-old could get in and out of the house without help. The project included new outside landscaping, relocation of an outdoor shed to another place in the yard, replacement of the roof, and repainting and patching the walls in most of the interior rooms as well as some other minor cosmetic changes.

We put together a crew of thirty people from the church—and fed them! To say it was a big job was an understatement. To accomplish our goal to complete the job in one day we used the following:

Plan: We brought the whole group together and split them into specialized teams. We assembled a materials list, a food list, and assigned specific responsibilities to people in a logical time-phased sequence of events. The counterbalance to this project was that we could not compromise safety in the name of expediency.

Do: Once we were satisfied with the plan we began to execute the project.

Check: We tracked our progress, checked our quality as the work was being done, monitored the consumption of our materials as we used them, tracked our conformance to schedule, and monitored work practices by all involved.

Act: We made corrections in terms of time, materials, reallocation of personal, quality conformance, and safety practices in real time.

The result was that we finished the project on time, on budget, with no injuries, and provided a quality product to our customer. The outward appearance of the product was a renovated house; the essence of the product was a ministry of compassion in the name of Christ to a real person with real needs in a real world.

– Joe Moleski, Campus Leader
Kensington Church

Chapter 7

Making Ministry Lean

"Space: the final frontier.
These are the voyages of the starship Enterprise.
Its five-year mission: to explore strange new worlds,
to seek out new life and new civilizations;
to boldly go where no man has gone before."

— Gene Rodenberry, 1966
Star Trek

We hope that we have successfully explained Lean and its connection to the twenty-first-century church. Now we have some choices. We could throw up our hands, contemplate our collective spiritual navel, and hope that somehow God will just work things out for us. Or, we could take control, bend circumstances to our will, and make something happen. Making anything happen is better than doing nothing, is it not? Does it really matter if we are focused as long as we are moving?

In a fallen world, we are hardwired to gravitate to one of those two choices, neither of which is appealing, godly, or effective. Fortunately, we have a third option. We can look around us, taking stock of what we possess and what we have to do. We can listen carefully for God's parental direction communicated so clearly and simply in the Bible and through people and the circumstances surrounding us. Then we can judiciously apply that which He's given us to accomplish that which He's asked of us.

God has called us and commissioned us; we must obey Him. We must go and do. It is not many years before our individual capabilities peak and begin to dwindle. We must take seriously how we use them. We naturally gravitate toward what

Dallas Willard calls "the gospel of sin management" in his book *The Divine Conspiracy*. We focus so hard on controlling our behaviors to some acceptable social level that we miss the big picture. We are expected to reach out; we are expected to go beyond our self-imposed horizon.

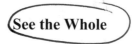

See the Whole

Lean uses the phrase "seeing the whole." It's a simple term, and can easily be overlooked. But seeing the whole will have profound consequences on your world. It means to back up and take an objective look at what you do, for whom you do it, and how you do it. Only after you have done this can you drill down into the details and make improvements by eliminating waste. Seeing the whole requires that you be honest, with yourself and those with whom you are engaged. It means to gather data and use it. It means to deny the big dog in the room his or her natural predisposition to control the outcome of whatever is going on. It requires strong leadership to make the right decisions and move God's church forward.

It is often said that perception is everything. This is convenient if we intend to provide to those to whom we minister with something that has been filtered to suit our biases and ignore their needs. To say perception is everything is not to simply say a cliché—it is to say a meaningless cliché. If we intend to actually respond to Him whom we serve, obey His requests, and do what He asks, we must see His world how it really is rather than how it is comfortable for us to perceive it. This is called reality and it may or may not bear any resemblance to our comfort level. We must see the big picture before we can see the details of the big picture—and not see it how we wish it was but how it really is. Jeremiah 17:9 (NIV) says, "The heart is deceitful above all things and beyond cure. Who can understand it?" Jeremiah does not say that the heart is deceitful only in certain circumstances. He says the heart is deceitful. This means that we will always filter what we see to interpret it in such a way as to conform to the biases of our heart. As we saw earlier, David Kinnaman, Gabe Lyons, Stanley Grenz, and Alan Hirsch, and others, have done an admirable job of describing the reality of the traditional church, and it's not a comfortable picture.

The first requirement to implement Lean is to learn to think differently. Everything we do and everything we think is fair game. It is important that we check our natural predisposition toward judgment at the door. We must think in terms of value-adding and non-value-adding activities. The Bible will be our standard for the issues of right and wrong and for issues of truth and untruth. We must muster the courage to be vulnerable and exposed to new thoughts and methods. We must be willing to live outside our comfort zones—to break away from having always done it "this way." Thinking differently is difficult—but it will be easier if we keep in mind that always having done it this way is largely responsible for getting us into this troubled place. Once we learn to see the reality of where we find ourselves, we can take action to change what we are doing. For discussion, we employ the following thought process:

- To know God is to see His reality →
- To see God's reality is to know God's values →
- To know God's values is to see how God values us →
- To know how God values us is to know our mission in this life →
- To know our mission in this life is to know God's present and future community →
- To know God's present and future community is to know our relationship to that community →
- To know our relationship to that community is to serve that community →
- To serve our community is to respond to God's values →
- To respond to God's values is to become more like Jesus Christ →
- To become more like Jesus Christ is to engage in the things that continually transform ourselves, our culture, and those we serve, and to respond to a changing world around us →
- As we engage in transformation, we will avoid those things that do not directly contribute to that goal.

When we objectively ask ourselves the questions, "What contributes directly to the transformation process and what does not?" and, "Do our efforts conform to our Lord's charter or are they counterproductive?" chances are the answers are mixed at best. It is these deficiencies we must address.

See the Scriptural Historicity of Lean

There are ample references in the Bible admonishing us to lean up. Here are a couple of them. The author of Hebrews (12:1 NIV) instructs: "Let us throw off everything that hinders and the sin that so easily entangles, and let us run with perseverance the race marked out for us." In Jeremiah 5:27–31, God refers to Jerusalem and His people as "'cages full of birds, their houses are full of deceit; they have become rich and powerful and have grown fat and sleek. Their evil deeds have no limit; they do not plead the case of the fatherless to win it, they do not defend the rights of the poor. Should I not punish them for this?' declares the LORD. 'Should I not avenge myself on such a nation as this? A horrible and shocking thing has happened in the land: The prophets prophesy lies, the priests rule by their own authority, and my people love it this way.'" (NIV).

Lean ministry is important today because it has been important from the beginning. Jesus didn't set Himself up in a central location and expect the people to come to Him. He went to them and He didn't carry a lot of baggage, neither material nor human.

See the Precedent: The Original Twelve Disciples
This book is all about simple questions and simple logic. Ask yourself the simple question, "Why did Jesus choose twelve disciples?" We have all heard sermons on the subject. The two principal themes are that there were twelve tribes of Israel and that Jesus picked a healthy mix of diverse personalities.

Since Jesus was fully God incarnate, He knew exactly what to do. He knew whom to choose, what personality strengths and weaknesses He needed to mix, and how many people to start with. Jesus knew that a number of different personalities would better reach the populace than just one or two personalities—much like many different Bible-teaching churches are needed to reach the many different cultures that need to hear the gospel.

Jesus did not minister to large groups at first. He first established a structured organization and began to mold it. Before He ministered to the multitudes He ministered to the seventy and then distilled out twelve into which to pour Himself for deep discipleship. Finally He chose Peter, James, and John in whom to invest Himself even further. They, with the remaining eight (and one substitute Jesus pulled off the bench), developed subordinate disciples who developed other subordinate disciples.

If twelve was good, why not one hundred and twelve? If we think like the twenty-first-century church, one hundred and twelve would have been much better—or even one thousand and twelve. We think Jesus' ministry was the original Lean Enterprise. We think Jesus chose twelve disciples simply because He knew twelve disciples would work best. Eleven would have been too few (not meeting the customer's needs) and thirteen would have been too many (overproducing). Lean says we use enough resources to make or provide only what the customer needs when the customer needs it—so Jesus' personal ministry on earth was the first Lean Enterprise. God incarnate knew exactly which resources to assemble to form the Original *Kaizen* Dream Team.

Jesus' original team was somewhat analogous to our present-day football kickoff team. Within that special team of eleven players we have two job descriptions. One kicks the ball, and the other ten establish field position for an assault on the receiving team. The kicker kicks the ball and runs to the sidelines—his job is over. The other ten run downfield and do their best to contain the ball carrier. Then the offense comes onto the field and mounts a concerted attack using more diverse job descriptions.

In Jesus' case, He had Judas put the ball in play, so to speak, and then run off the field. The other eleven ran downfield and established favorable field position. In football, we would like our team to advance the ball, but it moves forward and backward and sometimes we lose the game. The Original *Kaizen* Dream Team had complementary strengths that overcame their natural weaknesses. Each member, taken individually, could not advance the ball. But taken as a group they were a team of perfectly complementary talents—the original efforts of which advanced the ball for 2,000 years. Unlike the football analogy, The Original Dream Team could not lose. Jesus was Lean; His organization was Lean; His organization was formatted based on the reality in which they found themselves. This same approach can be used to help us examine, accept, and respond to a real world just as the original Twelve did.

See Ourselves as Others See Us
In recent years progressive church leadership has sought to make Christianity more attractive to those they call *seekers*. Worship formats, music styles, and dress codes have been reformatted to appeal to the seeker. The intent of these changes has been to make church attendance less threatening—or at least minimally offensive—to the seeker.

Chapter 3 should lay to rest any thoughts we might have that Christianity-at-large has anything attractive to offer the postmodern seeker. If their view is, "Christianity teaches the same basic principles as most other world religions," we shouldn't be surprised if they choose something that's more comfortable to them. If we think we are attractive because we know the truth we are making a mistake. There is no direct connection between knowing the truth and being attractive to those who do not. And we certainly never will be attractive if we filter what we believe through a series of bad or unattractive behaviors.

See Our Fundamental Character
Most readers have probably been in evangelical churches much of their lives. Many of us have been in leadership positions many of those years. It is a painful thing to say that the deeply godly, courageous, and strong leader is a rarity in our world. Most of us are good men or women who love our spouses and our children. We help out in church and conform more or less to being nice people. Most of us think this is an honorable label and something to aspire to—"evangelical nice."

In a number of his books, John Eldredge discusses the feminization of the church. He does this not to disparage the fairer sex, as some of his critics have suggested. He does it to call our attention to the fact that our primary visible characteristic is how nice we are. By becoming just so incredibly nice we deny the totality of our nature and become unbalanced. Certainly we must be loving, compassionate, and helpful, but our primary calling is to do battle as the weapons we were created to be. Our role is to glorify God and damage our enemy by transforming disciples. To do so we have to put ourselves in harm's way. We have to go onto the enemy's turf—he is certainly willing to come onto ours!

Evangelical nice lacks passion and authenticity. Propriety overrides honesty in evangelical nice. It robs one of spontaneity because one is forever censoring oneself and playing it safe. Evangelical nice robs one of spiritual and personal growth because its goal is one-dimensional. It does not allow Jesus Christ to pull us into our inner wounds and conflicts. It does not allow us to say the words "No" or "We must" or "You must do this."

Evangelical nice depends on maintaining an antiseptic environment, free from pain, controversy, or misunderstandings. God forbid that we should ever have a misunderstanding in the church because feelings might be hurt. It describes a posture of defense and avoidance. Evangelical nice produces neutral and uninspiring Christians—cookies cut from the same dough using the same cutter. It focuses inward on self and not outward on self-abandonment. Honest anger is more welcome to God than insincere smiles and handshakes—the Psalms are full of full-on emotional expressions, including anger from the "man after my own heart".

Nice and kind are two different things. We can be kind without being nice and we can be nice without being kind. Kindness is a character attribute issuing directly from God. Kindness is part of His nature and part of His image reflected in us. Kindness is driven by love and is compatible with transformed believers. It is linked to compassion and implies a compassionate response. Kindness is a fruit of the Spirit that we should all seek to harvest.

Nowhere does the Bible tell us to be nice. David was called a man after God's own heart. He wasn't nice. He was a murderer and an adulterer, among other things. He was kind, but he wasn't nice. Elijah was a godly man. But he killed 450 priests of Baal with a sword because it was the right thing to do. Anyone who has read the Epistles would certainly not call Paul nice. He was straightforward and courageous to the point of being rude. But he told the truth. Peter combines Paul's rudeness with rash and impulsive behavior. If Peter were alive today he would probably be medicated or sent to anger management classes. Matthew was a tax collector—not considered nice in biblical times, or today for that matter. Abraham was a manipulator and a schemer—not nice. But God made him the Father of Nations. James and John both had attitude issues—not nice, but Jesus loved them dearly. As for the women—how about Rahab, Esther, and Ruth? The Bible does not say they were nice people. In fact, they were manipulative and conspiratorial. But they were women who made things happen.

These, and many more examples, have something in common, and it is not "nice." They were bold leaders who made things happen, and God recorded their names for posterity. God chose those and other people because they had courage and didn't worry about keeping things in balance. They were willing to cause an upset in the world around them. It is doubtful that Martin Luther was thought of as a nice man.

The word "nice" is not compatible with the word "warrior." Neither is it compatible with any sentence ending with the words "…made things happen."

See Our Mission
Because they obeyed Him, God used the people mentioned above to glorify Him and to damage our enemy Satan. Our mission is no different than theirs. The details may be different, but the concept is the same. Empowered by God's Spirit, we are called to make things happen. We glorify God and damage the enemy through transformed lives. The mission of the church is to ensure that optimum conditions exist for effective flow of God's transformation process and for our spiritual DNA to flourish.

As we said, we are engaged in the mother of all battles—every day and all day long it never lets up. In this eternal contest we are either warfighters on the front lines or we are those who the fighters —there is no third option. As warfighters, we must be as light and fast as possible. As those who support warfighters, we must do everything in our power to provide them what they need when they need it. It is important that you determine which one of these roles you are meant to play.

If you have any question about which role you fill, take a look at 2 Samuel 23:8–16. The writer of 2 Samuel is describing David's mighty men, three of them in particular: Josheb-Basshebeth, Eleazar, and Shammah. To get the full impact you must read the whole passage. For now, verses 11 and 12 best provide a mirror to the world in which we live.

When the Philistines banded together at a place where there was a field full of lentils, Israel's troops fled from them. But Shammah took his stand in the middle of the field. He defended it and struck the Philistines down, and the Lord brought about a great victory. (NIV)

Contrast the pastoral scene of the farmer's field in which Shammah took his stand with the carnage that surrounded him as he struck down man after man with sword and spear—alone. The contrast is stark—much like the world in which we find ourselves today. Outwardly we strive to maintain a pastoral environment. We seek peace, stability, and tranquility while all around us the battle rages and the blood flows. Shammah was a warfighter.

If you do not look like one of David's mighty men, you are not a warfighter—your job is to support the warfighters. Within these two primary roles there are sub-categories of roles for both. They are called spiritual gifts. God, in His wisdom, has provided a perfect number of, and a perfect balance of, spiritual gifts to advance His battle (Romans 12; 1 Corinthians 7; 12; 14; 1 Peter 4). The word *perfect* is chosen for a reason—because His choices are perfect. Having been given these gifts, it is our responsibility to understand and fulfill the unique role that God has chosen for each of us.

See the Church as God Sees It

Churches manifest as many outward appearances as there are groups of people to conceive of them. This is well and good, but there is a definable essence common to all churches representing the Bride of Christ.

Many churches assume they are functional organs of transformation if they conform to the following equation:

Church = (a place) + (established positions) + (defined programs)

Where:
A *place* is a centrally located building, generally somewhat ornate.

Established positions are an elder or deacon board, some form of government, and dedicated staff persons, Sunday school teachers, and committee chairpersons.
Defined programs are the Sunday service, Sunday school, Awana, an Easter cantata, and a children's Christmas program, among others.

But this does not necessarily make up a well-functioning church—let alone a Lean church. The church has been entrusted with the process of transformation

(Colossians 1:28–29). And, whether you think the church must make something happen, or wait for God to make something happen to which the church must respond, we all must agree that the church must not be a barrier to transformation. The church should provide the opportunity for transformation to flow by minimizing waste in the process. To transform lives and damage the enemy, the church must not do things that do not contribute directly to the transformation process…and, in the venue where the transformation process is occurring.

A church should be a lean, mean, fighting machine and should be tailored to fight effectively on the battleground where it finds itself. The terrain will determine what the church looks like—there is no unilaterally exportable model. Any and all of its programs, positions, and governments should be tailored to generate results for the unique people group being transformed. It must have rapid response capability, flexibility, and activities or programs tailored to meet varied and emerging needs.

The following equation describes this essence:

Church = (a community of believers) + (small fellowship groups) + (flexible programs)

Where:

A *community of believers* is a group of Christ-following persons of any background or ethnicity living in limnality with the world around it. They are sensitive to the culture both inside and outside their community that God has given them for ministry and are establishing relationships with those groups.

Small fellowship groups are comprised of ten or twelve persons having a known and clearly understood mix of spiritual gifts, each person engaged in intimate fellowship with the other members on a regular basis. The group shares joys and sorrows and provides love, encouragement, and discipline when needed. It is equipped for every potentiality but uses only those tools necessary to reach the field around them; each member learning and growing from the diverse strengths of the other members; all small groups being directly linked, with accountability, to the greater congregation of which they are a part.

Flexible programs are not so entrenched or rigid as to prevent rapid and effective response to changes in the world where the church finds itself. Flexible programs will accommodate the church's need to live in limnality with that world. These programs will have mobility to move throughout the community rather than expecting the community to come to the church. A culture of continuous improvement must be inculcated into the programs so that the people nearest to the needs may constantly improve their responses to those needs.

These days we are all familiar with video footage of soldiers deploying to Iraq or Afghanistan. As they board the plane they are laden with equipment and tools to meet every conceivable need. They have weapons, ammunition, medical supplies, extra food, extra water, and pieces of crew-served weapons. They can hardly breathe carrying 120+ pounds of equipment, let alone move swiftly and surely to cause damage to the enemy. They are carrying so much gear they can hardly walk. Each soldier carries his share of specialized equipment—some having common items and some having different items. As individuals they are inadequate but as a group they are fully equipped to meet any eventuality—much like God has equipped His Bride with all the tools she needs. But those soldiers will not use all that equipment at the same time. If they plan to fight like that they will surely fail. Instead they will select the tools they need to respond to the problems facing them as those problems evolve. When they go into battle they will shed every last ounce of equipment they do not absolutely need to move as light and as fast as possible. Their very lives are dependent upon maximum mobility and flexibility. In the same way, an effective church must be formatted to carry out God's mission of transformation on the terrain where it finds itself. You may call it a battle or you may call it a race, as Paul does in 1 Corinthians 9:24 and as the writer of Hebrews does in Hebrews 12:1. No matter—it's the same concept. To accomplish our mission we must be light, fast, and flexible.

Envision a Lean Church

Being a visionary is a fundamental requirement of effective leadership. We must see the reality of God's local church as it is, but we must also have a vision of His local church as it should be. If we do not or cannot have that vision, we cannot lead His local church toward realizing change.

We will not know if His local church is lean without a detailed assessment of its performance characteristics relative to the transformation process, but here are some beatitudes that will give us a conceptual picture of what that vision could look like. It may help us to jumpstart our vision about the type of church that will effectively fight the battle in which we are all engaged. It is informal, but informal is better than no assessment at all. Ask yourself if the church where you serve has the following attributes. If you are in a church leadership position, try to put yourself in the position of the person on the other side of the pulpit.

NOT THIS	BUT THIS
A religion or denomination	Following Christ as his disciple
Focusing our spiritual life on Sundays	Developing a 24/7 lifestyle
Focusing our spiritual life in the "temple"	Living all of life under His Lordship
Worshipping once a week for two hours	Worshipping all week in all that we do
Content just to be forgiven	Actively embracing God's agenda
Spectators and pew warmers	Actively giving and receiving within an organic system
Tied to traditions given "once-and-for-all"	Seek and follow His leadership and change as needed
People-pleasers	God-pleasers
Program-oriented	Process-oriented
Nurseries to care for spiritual babies	Reproductive spiritual "orchards"
Forgiven frogs	Budding princes and princesses
Pastoral-care dependency	Congregational-care interdependency
Alpha-male directed	Alpha and Omega-directed by a team of qualified elders
Freedom from accountability	Freedom through accountability
No continuing education and training	Continual education and training
Sacred/secular dichotomy	Lordship over all areas of life
Undiscipled, sterile church leaders	Disciples, fruitful ministry leaders
Discipleship as an initial follow-up course	Transformation as an intentional life-long purpose
Disconnected from the community	Living in limnality with the community
Impersonal feel of shoulder-to-shoulder	Personal feel of face-to-face
One-way verbal telling	Involved by: asking, listening, answering, talking, showing
Just large group meetings	A balance of large & small groups
Just committed to the local church	Committed to the Kingdom and the Church-at-large
Only delighting in being saved	Also delighting in becoming like Christ
Hiding the truth to maintain an image	Transparency to maintain integrity
Hearers of the Word who know about God	Doers of the Word who know God

Figure 7.1: Church Assessment

See Your People Group

The tribal lines have been redrawn within Christianity as well as without. Within Christianity we are still Swedish Baptists, German Lutherans, or Polish Catholics, but the lines describing ethnicity, orthodoxy, and theology have become more fluid. Outside Christianity it becomes staggeringly complex because we remove the Metanarrative of mankind, the doctrine of grace, and the existence of a central truth. It will be nigh impossible to provide your people group the opportunity for transformation without qualifying them with the most empirical and objective process you can find.

At a minimum you should know their:
- Age
- Gender
- Professional level
- Socioeconomic status
- Education level

Additional helpful information would be:
- Marital status
- Former church affiliation and exposure
- Position on the timeline of transformation
- Music orientation
- Language
- Values

The processes with which a particular believer or group of believers can identify and use for growth will look very different from those that are effective with other people groups, cultures, and socioeconomic strata. The external characteristics of transformation processes that are effective in a white, upper-middle class church family in a small Midwestern city will be different than the external characteristics from those that are effective in an inner-city Mexico City church family. Believers within these two diverse examples are created in the image of God and have the same fundamental needs for salvation and development, but will respond differently to different transformation programs. This is an extreme example and easy to see. What is not so easy to see are the different sub-groups resident within an already established congregation.

You will have to ask questions and gather information about those sub-groups for your church to format itself to provide the maximum opportunity for transformation. You will have to go into the community and discover its needs, biases, and processes. Ask your churchgoers why they come to church and why they are involved in your congregation or why they avoid involvement. In conversation with those who do not go to church, ask them why they do not come to church and what it would take to get them involved in your congregation or what you could take to them. If biblical compromise will not occur in order to make such changes, by all means make them. Paul did (1 Corinthians 9:21–23).

Establish Leadership Consensus
If you have a vision of what your church can become, and God has provided you the courage to make a decision to implement change, you must garner the support of your key stakeholders before you attempt to communicate your vision to those whom you lead. Leadership consensus is critical.

Disagreement during the consensus-building process is not only permissible—it is healthy and encouraged. It is unrealistic and naïve to think that any single individual has all the answers. Each individual has part of the answer, and disagreement is a foregone conclusion. This is how steel sharpens steel.

The word "confrontation" has taken on a negative connotation in recent years. But it's just a word. In this case it should be attached to a positive, rather than a negative, definition. You cannot achieve consensus without confrontation. That's what leaders do—they confront issues, situations, and problems. Sometimes they are required to confront each other. With the door to the conference room closed, you may disagree on any and all subjects. You must stop somewhere short of banging your shoe on the table like Nikita Khrushchev at the U.N. in 1960.

When the conference room door opens and you exit, your team must be aligned. You must be in agreement as to your vision and the process for achieving your vision. You must agree on both the reality of your present position and the position you hope to achieve. Any disagreement that exits the conference room with you will act like a cancer in your congregation and disproportionately inhibit your ability to make change.

Understand and Accept God's Values as Your Own

Listen to the Voice of the Customer (VOC)
The VOC captures the requirements and feedback from the customer in order to provide the best possible service and product quality. The VOC process captures what the customer wants and how and when we should provide it. The VOC facilitates responsiveness and innovation to meet changing requirements over time. The VOC uses a variety of tools: Direct discussion, interviews, surveys, focus groups, written feedback, direct observation, failure information, field reports, and complaints.

This sounds a lot like our Christian Bible, does it not? What else is our Bible if not the VOC? We established earlier that God is not a customer because He has no needs. Though not a customer, He is the initiator and the receiver of everything that did exist, exists now, or will exist in the future. He is the reason for our existence. It is Him whom we serve. His values may be summed up in a single statement: we must glorify Him and obey Him.

Establish Your Baseline Position

Leadership's Role

By now you have come a long way toward seeing the whole and it is time to begin working. Your first order of business is to establish a baseline understanding of your church's strengths and weaknesses. (For an example of a completed baseline analysis, see Appendix B: Lean Analysis—Highland Community Church, Wausau, WI.)

To do this you must have help because even though you may be acting in a position of senior leadership, you can easily become your greatest hindrance. It is time to delegate some responsibilities to an array of specialists that you must assemble. But before you assemble and charter a team you must understand your role as leader.

Your job as a leader is to first have a vision and then set clear, understandable goals representing your vision. You must establish the conceptual expectations of the team but you must not, under any circumstances, give them the answer they are supposed to arrive at. After all, if the answer is so obvious, why would you need a team? You must set timelines for reporting progress and establish a reporting method that makes it easy for the team to communicate to the leadership. You must set a realistic completion date for whatever project you have set your team to work on; their completion date cannot be open-ended. Then you must do the hardest thing of all—you must get your hands off the team and let them work.

Select and Charter the Team

Your Lean team must be carefully chosen. There is no preset number of members but you want as few as possible to still get the job done. You must select people that possess the talent, motivation, courage, and dedication to produce an honest assessment of your church's value-added and non-value-added activities. Remember that no single team member will have all the answers. Once selected, the team must be chartered using a written document containing, at a minimum, the following information:

- **Roles and Responsibilities**. You must establish and communicate specific roles and responsibilities for each member of the team. The strength of team-based problem solving is in the cross-functional nature of the specialties that are represented. Each team member has part of the answer or understands how to get part of the answer. So, each member must understand why he or she has been chosen. You must appoint a team leader whose role it is to keep the team on track, and that team leader must understand that he or she is only first among equals and does not have veto power over any recommendations.

- **Problem Statement.** You must communicate the compelling reasons for embarking on this project to eliminate waste. You must explain to the team how this project is linked to your church's key goals and objectives. You must give them some roughly estimated order of magnitude of expected improvement. Then your team must write a statement specifically defining the problem. Where and when does it occur? What is its extent? Is it measureable?

- **Goal Statement.** The improvement opportunity must be stated in simple, straightforward language. An acronym to help write the goal statement is SMART. Test the goal statement to see if: It is *S*pecific; it is *M*easureable; it is *A*ttainable; it is *R*elevant; and, if it is *T*ime-bound. If it meets these criteria, you have established a goal that your team can work with.

- **Project Scope.** You and your team must establish what is inside as well as outside the scope of the project. You must determine and communicate which elements of your church's transformation processes are within the purview of the team's charter as well as those that are not. Without clear boundaries for project scope, projects tend to creep and become too large and sometimes unmanageable. Do not attempt to boil the ocean.

- **Milestones.** You must set realistic milestone and completion dates. Without milestone dates and a completion date the team will labor on in perpetuity, achieving little, and become disheartened. You need regular update reports to determine if the team is focused, making progress, and on schedule.

- **Communication Plan.** You must establish the dynamics of the communication plan to keep you and other key stakeholders updated and when to involve ad hoc subject matter experts. They need to know which content must be communicated, namely, who, what, when, where, why, and how?

- **Counterbalance.** The team needs is a clear and simple understanding of the project counterbalance. The counterbalance to any project is something that cannot be compromised in the interest of expediency. Sometimes the counterbalance is not so easy to see when examining intangible processes like those of your church, but it's there. The highest level counterbalance in your church's transformation processes is truth. Truth cannot be compromised in the interest of expediency. There may be one counterbalance or there may be several, depending on the situation.

All of this chartering sounds like a lot of unnecessary activity to simply explain your expectations to the team—but it is necessary. In practice, if the champion, process owner, and team leader are focused, the above process should take about an hour. Once the charter is complete, and all members understand their roles, the team will meet at predetermined times, analyze the process and problems, make a justifiable recommendation, and execute that recommendation at the direction of the leadership. Once the resolution has been executed, the team tracks performance using as simple a metric as possible.

Benchmark a Lean Church
There is no reason to re-create the wheel if you don't have to. You should do what others do if those methods are, in fact, exportable. Even though no two churches are alike, there are churches similar enough to benchmark. Some of these may have experienced problems like yours and have taken steps to solve them. It is possible that you could export their methods to your church and tailor them to your specific needs.

Map Your Processes
Process maps and flowcharts are graphical representations of otherwise intangible processes. Steps in a process are shown with symbolic shapes and the flow is indicated with arrows connecting the symbols. You may have many church programs in play at any time, but you will have a group of core processes representing the main focus of the church. It may be six, eight, or ten programs, but unless you are a very unusual church, it's probably not more than this. Flowcharts are very useful to show how a process currently functions as well as how it could ideally function. They help you to see whether the processes are logical; they uncover problems or miscommunications; they define the boundaries of a process; and they develop a common base of knowledge to enable the team to visualize an entire process and identify areas of value and waste.

- **High-Level Process map.** High-level flowcharts map only the major steps in a process and provide a good overview. They help you see the big picture and point you in the general direction of where you should continue to look for opportunities.

- **As-Is Process Map.** An as-is process map takes the high-level map to the next level of detail and gives a picture of your processes as they currently are. It is the starting point to understanding how a process is running and becomes the basis for drawing the should-be map.

- **Should-Be Process Map.** The should-be map is the natural product of the as-is map. It shows how we want the new and improved version of a process to run based on everything being done right the first time.

Plot a Cause and Effect Matrix (C&E)

After you have mapped your processes to a level of detail showing individual process inputs, you can use a C&E matrix to compare key process input variables (KPIVs) to key process output variables (KPOVs).

- **Key Process Input Variables (KPIVs):** These are what you do in the church to help facilitate transformation in terms of clearly defined church programs and activities.
- **Key Process Output Variables or Expectations (KPOVs):** These are your clearly defined expectations or hoped-for outcomes and represent developmental impact on the spiritual DNA of the congregation.

Unfortunately, you cannot jump straight to a C&E matrix without going through the process-mapping exercises mentioned earlier. But, once having done that, the C&E matrix assigns objective criteria to otherwise subjective elements of your church life so you can actually measure how effective you are. The C&E matrix is the start of getting some real answers as to which church programs are more or less effective based on your expected or hoped-for outcomes.

Apply a Resource Allocation Analysis

Once you know which of your church programs most positively affect your expected outputs you must determine how much it costs to get these results (or non-results). Determining cost per expected outcome is critical because you have an infinite task to accomplish but your resources are finite. You must know where your resources are being spent if you wish to use them more effectively. Broad categories are:

- Paid staff time
- Unpaid and volunteer staff time
- IT costs
- Utilities and other buildings and grounds costs
- Debt service on a mortgage if you still have one

Map Your Value Streams

Now the term "value stream mapping" becomes meaningful. Value stream mapping is like process mapping, but the value stream map contains empirical data to qualify and quantify both value-added and non-value-added activities.

Each one of your church's core programs will have a process of its own by which it is executed. Each of those processes represents a stream of value-added and non-value-added activities, and each of those value streams consumes some measure of your precious resources.

Value stream mapping these processes identifies each task that is performed in sequence, from the beginning to the end of the process, and applies empirical data to each of those steps, as appropriate to define value and waste. Sometimes things just happen haphazardly, or not at all—or different people use different processes to accomplish the same end. A major benefit of creating a value stream map is the learning that naturally occurs when people try to determine how things actually get done.

To map your value streams you must choose a starting point. By now you have a very good idea of both the effectiveness (the relative impact that you achieve) and the efficiency (how much it costs you per unit impact) for your church's core programs. In fact, if you've done due diligence to the analysis thus far you have a great deal of data to use to begin drilling deeper and looking for opportunities to eliminate waste. Your starting point may be the Sunday service or the singles ministry. It may be the women's Bible study or your small group program. The starting point will be different for each church.

Whatever your situation, pick whichever core processes that the C&E matrix and the resource allocation analysis have shown to be either the most important or the most problematic to your church.

The value stream map comes in two forms—the current-state and the future-state.

- **Current-State Value Stream Map.** The current-state value stream map shows value and waste within a process as it currently exists. This map will contain as much empirical data as you need to make decisions—such as wait times for people and information, redundancies, excessive handling or handoffs, cycle times for both preparation and execution, activities or loops that go nowhere, and activities used to correct deficiencies.

- **Future-State Value Stream Map.** The future-state value stream map is the current-state map redrawn to show those areas of waste having been removed or corrected. The future-state map shows your target—what you are hoping to achieve through the improvement activities of the team. The difference between the current-state and the future-state maps is, of course, savings. The savings will come in the form of dollars, time, and quality improvement. With Lean, an improvement in the quality of the product always results in a reduction of the cost of a product.

Conduct Root Cause Analyses (RCA)

By now you will be seeing what you will want to call "problems" and will be asking yourself why these problems repeatedly occur. What we call problems are very often not problems at all; they are merely symptoms of problems, the root cause of which needs to be discovered before you can correct it. In fact, it is unusual for anyone to immediately see the root cause of a given problem without doing some type of RCA.

There are a number of very effective RCA techniques, but some of them are complex and can become frustrating to people who do not use them on a regular basis. The simplest, and one of the most effective, is something called the "5 Whys Analysis." The 5 Whys Analysis allows you to get to the root cause of a problem fairly quickly by repeatedly asking the question, "Why did this happen?" This makes it possible to peel away the layers of symptoms to identify root causes. It may take you six repetitions or you may get the answer in four, but five is a good rule of thumb – each repetition taking you one level deeper until you get to the root cause.

Draw Conclusions as to Where to Start

By this point your team has used structured and proven tools to systematically and deliberately reduce a large amorphous organization with complex, and sometimes confusing, processes to something that you can see, clearly understand, and begin to change for the better. You now know:

- The relative impact of each of your church's core programs.
- The cost-effectiveness of each of your church's core programs.
- Areas of waste within each of your church's core programs.
- Root causes of problems that just don't seem to go away.

The Dynamics of Change

It bears mentioning that by this point that a great deal of work has been done and you still haven't actually changed anything. But cultural and organizational change is difficult, and without this prep work it will be impossible to guarantee lasting change. "When can I actually *do* something?" you cry plaintively. "When can I actually *make* some improvement?" you implore. Well, you are in luck— you can start right after a few words on the dynamics of change.

First, sum it up by saying change is hard. Without going through the aforementioned process the big dog will continue to have his or her way just like it's always been. Now everyone knows where to start and why they need to start there. Old habits die hard in all organizations, especially those with a 1700-year entrenched culture. You want change? Be careful what you wish for. The fact that you have put in this much work and still haven't changed anything should give you a very strong clue as to why organizations do not change easily. It is sad to say that most organizations do not feel the need to change until they find themselves in crisis and are presented with a picture of clear and present danger. Then it is often too late. Because by the time the problem is visible to everyone they have achieved a level of downward momentum too great to overcome. It behooves organizations to buy into a vision of change and improvement before their situation becomes critical.

Very few people actually thrive on change—perhaps one in a hundred. The remaining ninety-nine may say they do because it's popular to say so. But when it comes down to actually doing things differently, most are immobilized and strive as hard as they can to maintain their static position. Unfortunately, there is no such thing as a static position. Individuals, as well as organizations, are either moving forward or falling behind. Static is a self-serving illusion requiring strong leadership to overcome.

If your church does not have strong leadership you should consider making no changes until such leadership is in place. But let's say that you have followed all the rules and have assembled the team and gathered data and done the proper RCAs. The changes that you must make are clear and you have consensus as to how to move forward. If you do not have the leadership in place to make the changes and ensure the changes are carried out and maintained, you can set yourself back years. You can create an environment far more hostile to change than the one in which you find yourself now.

Most organizations have a truly impressive ability to rebound to their original condition and behaviors once the pressure to change has been relieved. All organizations, including churches, have a unique corporate culture that is the sum of all the people in that organization—and nearly all of those people resist change. The culture is entrenched, having been developed over time for solid reasons—be they good or bad reasons.

In his book *Leading Change*, Harvard professor John P. Kotter defines eight critical steps when making changes:

1) Identify a sense of urgency as to why change is needed.
2) Have the support of leadership—and several layers of leadership for that matter.
3) Compose a compelling vision that can be articulated in five minutes or less.
4) Over-communicate the vision; you can never communicate it enough.
5) Make certain all obstacles are removed and ensure that all key people are truly on board.
6) Celebrate short-term wins along the way.
7) Be careful not to celebrate ultimate victory too soon. True changes take years to become part of an organization's DNA.
8) Anchor changes in the corporation's culture.

Respond to the Pull of Jesus Christ

To develop the future-state of your transformation processes into something that can be both effective and efficient you must reduce the batch size and make your processes flow in response to pull. Push is the opposite of pull. Push happens when the church decides to do something that pushes value to the customer before the customer has asked for it or has demonstrated a need—making the church unable to glorify God.

Reduce the Batch Size
If you have bought into the discussion of Lean ministry to this point, a rather shocking conclusion should absolutely leap off the page. It is this: the larger the church, the more difficult the church's role in individual transformation becomes. The larger the church, the more predisposed we are to processing people in batches. The more we process people in batches, the less likely we are of actually meeting anyone's specific need. We cannot push people toward Jesus. We cannot push transformation on people who are not ready to accept it. Jesus pulls all people toward Himself. It is our job to help facilitate the flow of the transformation process in response to that pull—when He exerts the pull. This cannot be done either effectively or efficiently in large batches.

An exhaustive discussion of pull and how to reduce the batch size as it applies to all church programs is beyond the scope of this book. Instead we offer you a simple example that may help you see the possibilities and accept some realities in principle that will guide you.

The Sunday service in most churches is a good example of pushing a large batch through a common process. In most churches, the Sunday service is designed to teach. Teaching is good because Jesus was a teacher. We have already said that we think teaching and learning should be first among equals within the eight elements of spiritual DNA in each believer. We should be lifelong Christian learners, and we need teachers to help us.

In most churches, the Sunday service is one of the least effective core programs in terms of transformation impact on believers' DNA. It is also, normally, one of the most cost-ineffective programs we have in the church. This is what we call, in the world of change management, an opportunity—for improvement.

Many churches have small groups. Small groups are designed to take the individual believer deeper and further into the transformation process. In contrast to the Sunday service, small groups are one of the most effective of the church's programs in terms of impact on believers' DNA. Small groups are also one of the most cost-effective programs, costing very little to form, administer, and execute. This is another example of what we call, in the world of change management, an opportunity—to capitalize on a success.

We have the opportunity to create a very strong dynamic and a dependable pull system by simply linking these two generally freestanding programs together, thus maximizing the impact of both.

How we see the Sunday service will determine how we employ what takes place there in our lives. Senior pastors and denominational leadership see the Sunday service differently than the average person on the other side of the pulpit. Professional evangelical clergy tend to see the Sunday service as an activity initiating the next seven-day period until Sunday rolls around again. They see it as a beginning. However, those sitting in the pews tend to see it as the culmination of the most recent seven-day period. For many of us, the act of going to church fulfills our worship and relational requirements. As long as we, on the other side of the pulpit, see the Sunday service this way it will remain as the end point—when, in fact, it should be the starting point.

For the Sunday service to act as a starting point, it must have something to start, and if we start something we have to complete something. To complete something we need structured follow-up and feedback. That's where the small groups come in. Most pastors have a large library of sermons and know well in advance what they will be preaching. Nearly all seasoned pastors preach sermons in series—each successive sermon building on its predecessor—while small groups most often choose their own subject matter and pursue it at their own pace. By directly linking the sermon series material to small groups and implementing a structured feedback system, shown in the graphic below, we have overcome the inherent weaknesses in one program, harnessed the inherent strengths in the other program, and made each of them more effective and efficient. They have become greater than the sum of their parts.

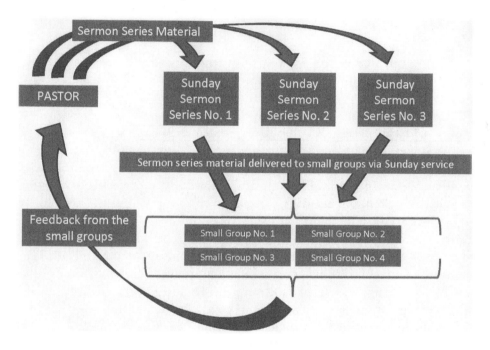

Figure 7.2: Linking the Sunday Service with Small Groups

This link would be further strengthened by providing each small group with a structured and anonymous feedback tool to the pastor. The feedback tool should be simple and quick but allow for ranking, rating, and making suggestions for the sermon material to be improved for the coming Sunday. If provided early enough in the week, the pastor can incorporate this valuable information into his forthcoming sermon.

By making this small change for the better we have functionally changed the Sunday service from what most of the congregation sees as an end point to a legitimate starting point for the coming week. By providing feedback to the pastor we have given him the opportunity to make quality corrections in the material for the coming week. We have given the congregation a voice to communicate what they need and to report what they have absorbed. We have reduced the batch size and thus facilitated some supercharged learning within the small groups. We have initiated flow in response to pull because now the small groups pull the Sunday sermon material based on what they heard and what they need rather than the sermon being pushed toward them in a void. We have changed the flow of energy from going into the Sunday service to issuing out of the Sunday service into a mechanism that can more effectively minister to each person. And it passes the Lean acid test by improving the quality while making the process easier for everyone involved.

Seek Perfection Through Continuous Improvement

Kaizen

In contrast to the usual emphasis on revolutionary, innovative change on an occasional basis, *kaizen* looks for uninterrupted, ongoing, incremental change. *Kaizen* is the continuous drive toward perfection. Perfection should be our goal, even though we know we cannot achieve it. We will always be flawed but Jesus was not. Jesus should be our perfect standard and his perfect behaviors and responses should be our behavioral goals.

Perfection means applying this Lean approach to other church core programs, involving more people in the effort, and revisiting areas that have already been improved. Perfection means applying the improvement activities described in this chapter on an ongoing basis—as a part of normal operations. No church will ever progress beyond the need to improve value for our Lord's through the elimination of waste. Just as individual renewal is an ongoing effort, so renewal of the church must be an ongoing effort.

Before we move on to a chapter-length treatment of leadership and *kaizen*, we want you to consider the subject of *kaizen* and involving your people very carefully. What we call *kaizen* is generally not done in the twenty-first-century church. In fact, most churches do not understand the concept. Many pastors and staffs do seek feedback from their congregations. But *kaizen* is not simply seeking feedback. *Kaizen* is employing the rank and file to accomplish goals that you otherwise cannot. What eventually results in sweeping change must evolve by gradual improvement rather than radical changes.

Kaizen is about empowering people in a structured environment. It is about assembling your subject matter experts and bringing them to bear on unresolved problems. It is about pushing accountability and responsibility downward in the organization to the lowest practical level (stress the word *practical*). It is about temporary appointment, not election, to teams and not about permanent membership on standing committees.

In our current evangelical culture, this will likely be the most difficult barrier to overcome. Church cultures and governments come in many forms. There are: oligarchies, social democracies, and benevolent dictatorships. Some use parliamentary procedure. Some pass sweeping changes with a quorum of less than 10% of the voting members while some require a majority vote. Within these diverse types of governments there are unions—yes, unions. Not formalized collective bargaining units but networks of people who make things happen or prevent things from happening. There are associations of people with special interests or disinterests. And, of course, there is the Old Guard—those who know best because they have been there the longest. These groups represent the smallest but most powerful part of the total congregation. The greatest quotient of the congregation is those people who do not fall into the above categories. These are the people we should be looking to for help and practical guidance. Whatever your church culture may be, it is generally true to say that a select few guide an unselected many in the twenty-first-century church. As a result, evangelicalism often makes decisions in a vacuum of input. What is ironic is that this truth exists in a culture that claims, at least since the Protestant Reformation, the priesthood of all believers.

If we have held your attention, and you have read through the book thus far, let us deliver the coup de grace. Lean cannot be implemented in an autocratic environment. Lean cannot be implemented without *kaizen*. *Kaizen* requires the involvement of people who seldom, if ever, get the opportunity to actually do something. Unless you are willing to selectively involve individuals from your congregation in the improvement process, do not even try it. You will do more damage than you can imagine.

Performance Measurements
Performance measurements are critical to progress for obvious reasons. Runners cannot run a race if they do not run against a clock and against their competitors' times. We cannot know who is ahead in the football game without a scoreboard. Airplanes will crash into mountains if they do not have an accurate and prominently displayed altimeter. Similarly, churches focusing on improvement cannot know if they are making progress without commonly understood, meaningful, and prominently displayed performance metrics.

Many of you remember sitting in church and seeing the board off to the side of the pulpit showing the week-on-week comparison of Sunday service attendance, Sunday school attendance, and weekly offerings. Those boards are mostly gone now. Frankly, they probably should be gone because they were for the most part meaningless. But the concept remains the same—we must track progress to know if we are actually making progress.

The two most common performance indicators in use today in the twenty-first-century evangelical church are 1) total number of members or attendees and 2) conformance to budget. Neither of these is directly linked to the church's mission—transformation of believers.

There is an argument against performance metrics in the church that goes something like this: "If we track our performance we have the opportunity to take false pride in the metrics and glorify ourselves rather than glorify God." This sounds very much like the tail wagging the dog. Indeed, that might give someone an opportunity to develop false pride. But false pride can manifest itself in anything we do and it makes no sense to not assemble the information because someone might misuse it.

Let us suggest some simple and meaningful performance metrics that, if tracked and prominently displayed, would be of great help to all members of the church— leaders and followers alike. Lean calls these publicly displayed performance metrics *glass walls* or *visual management*, meaning the leadership is willing to be transparent and publicly accountable for their actions.

- **Profile the Transformation Maturity of Your Congregation.** We can provide our congregation with a simple and clearly worded description of each of the stages in the transformation process and ask each person to place himself or herself on the continuum. Of course, those persons may lie and rank themselves greater or lesser than they actually are. But, studies continue to show that self-assessment methods are at least as accurate as external assessments—and often better.

- **Profile the Development of Your Congregation's Spiritual DNA.** We can provide simple definitions of each of the eight elements of spiritual DNA and ask the individual believer to rank himself or herself on a scale of 1–5 as to their development in each area.

- **Numbers of People in Small Groups.** We can simply track the number of people involved in a small group. Some churches already do this, but few directly link small group subject matter to the Sunday sermon. Linking small groups to the Sunday sermon with a closed loop feedback process, and tracking the number of people active in small groups, is a dependable measure of how many people the pastor is actually reaching on a deeper level.

- **Individual Contacts External to the Church.** The high-level process map of many traditional twenty-first-century evangelical churches will show that nearly all the programs are pointing inward toward the church's congregation. Few point outward in a functional way unless they are designated as a mission organization. It would be very helpful to know how many external contacts our congregation is making per unit time.

- **Number of Dollars or Percent of Budget Spent External to the Church.** As with the previous, if we intend to reach out, it will cost money. Most evangelical churches have missions budgets, but they are typically only reviewed during quarterly business meetings. We challenge any of you to recall a church where the missions budget was prominently and publicly displayed—or compared to internal expenditures.

These are a few simple performance metrics that could easily be assembled and tracked in a spreadsheet. The transparency provided by publicly displaying them will enhance the credibility of the leadership, provide a sense of involvement and impact among the regular members, and assist improvement teams and individuals as they make small changes for the better.

SPIRIT CHURCH
Applying the Principle of Value to Continuous Improvement

A simple, but effective, application of Lean comes from a church plant we will call Spirit Church, located in a small, struggling, Southern suburban town (the name and location are kept confidential to avoid calling attention to the church). This church has taken a courageous step by examining the value that their ministries do or do not provide to determine if their limited resources will allow all of their ministries to continue.

The church has a small but committed core group that is augmented by some volunteer help from other churches in the area. This core group recently reviewed the "kingdom value" of each of their ministries. The focus of this effort was to determine which of those ministries were reaching the people group that each program was designed to reach and whether there was demonstrable change in the lives of those people.

One popular ministry was a weekly tutoring program at a local school serving students with discipline problems or who were not demonstrating satisfactory academic progress. Spirit had long-standing support from the other churches in the area for this program. And, there could be no doubt that this was a good thing to do. But after almost two years of involvement with these students Spirit could see no significant change in many of them and observed little or no interest from the children's parents in reinforcing the work the tutors were doing.

The second important discovery to come out of their forthright and courageous examination was that they were not providing a meaningful learning or worship experience for the children of their regular attendees.

When they stepped back and evaluated these two areas of ministry, the core team determined that they were devoting their resources to something good but to an area of lesser value when considering God's priority of transformation in His children.

The core team made the difficult call to suspend the tutoring program and start a new children's Bible-based teaching program on Sunday mornings prior to the regular worship service. By shifting their volunteer resources from an area where little kingdom value was being observed to an area where children were more likely to have biblical principles reinforced by parents, Spirit Church hopes to see their efforts yield real life transformation.

In the spirit of continuous improvement, the pastor and his core team will review this new program and the value they hope for it to create, making adjustments along the way as necessary. It is very unusual to see a church stop doing a good thing in order to do something that will likely be an even better thing, especially when they have ample volunteer resources. The focus on continuous improvement to provide real value is serving Spirit Church and increasing the probability that it will become fully sustainable.

– Johnny Ervin,
LifeBridge Church

Chapter 8

Leadership and *Kaizen*

"You may be an ambassador to England or France,
You may like to gamble, you might like to dance,
You may be the heavyweight champion of the world,
You may be a socialite with a long string of pearls

But you're gonna have to serve somebody, yes indeed
You're gonna have to serve somebody,
Well, it may be the devil or it may be the Lord
But you're gonna have to serve somebody."

"Gotta Serve Somebody"
– Bob Dylan, 1979

Leadership

To understand how *kaizen* works, and how important it is, we must first understand leadership and its relationship to followership. Leaders lead and followers follow—but this broad definition can take many forms in many contexts. Many thousands of pages have been written on the subject of leadership, what it is, and how it works. They all reduce to the same common denominator. Leadership is getting a group of people to do something that they either cannot do or will not do as well without a leader. Leaders must first be followers but not all followers can become leaders.

To profile what effective leadership should look like, consider the Battle of Gettysburg and General Longstreet's assault on the Union Army at Cemetery Hill, Culp's Hill, and Little Round Top near Gettysburg, Pennsylvania during the first three days in July, 1863. How the forces were joined is a subject for another discussion. But, two large, opposing, armies met at the same place at the same time with the most terrible results in U.S. military history.

The Federal Army of the Potomac arrived more or less first and occupied favorable fighting positions. Lee's Army of Northern Virginia arrived tired, hungry, and poorly equipped compared to the Federals. Many of Lee's troops were without shoes. The Confederacy was forced to occupy the lower ground and fortune favored the Federals in all ways. But Lee felt that the devotion and courage of his seasoned men would prevail. He was wrong and his decision forever changed the direction of our Nation.

In those three days greater than 51,000 men were killed, wounded, or missing on both sides of the line. Although the war raged on for two more years, it was a decisive victory for the Union precipitating the South's retreat. Its terrible losses were a turning point in the war and from that point on, the South had to abandon its attempt to take the war to the North. Newt Gingrich and William Forstchen have written a book titled *Gettysburg: A Novel of the Civil War* in which the authors theorize what our country would be like had the outcome of one battle in our Nation's history been different. It makes for interesting reading.

The most studied action of one of the most studied battles in history is what has been called Pickett's Charge, but General Pickett was only one of the Confederate generals involved in the battle. The key player was General Longstreet. General Lee's request of General Longstreet called for 12,500 Confederate infantry to march uphill for over 1,000 yards in oppressive heat, laden with battle gear, into the face of withering artillery and then small arms and canister fire. The men knew they had a high probability of being struck down. As it turned out, that probability proved to be greater than 50%.

Yes, General Lee's decision was wrong. Yes, it resulted in unnecessary catastrophic losses on both sides. Yes, it broke the back of Confederate spirit and resistance. But it is not the result of the decisions made by Generals Lee and Longstreet that we use as an example—it is the quality of their leadership.

Ask yourself how Generals Lee and Longstreet got those 12,500 men to step off the line and willingly walk into that kind of carnage. As a leader, what would it take for you to send those men up that hill? As a follower, what would it take for you to step off the line? There are only two possible answers to these questions. The first is that the men feared General Lee more than they feared the enemy. The second answer is that they loved General Lee more than they feared the enemy and believed in a cause much greater than the value of their own lives. Students of history and leadership know the correct answer to be the latter.

This is leadership of a quality that should make strong men weep. Yet, it is only human leadership. How much more should we esteem the leadership and follow the guidance of our Heavenly Father with His perfect love toward His perfect plan?

Rear Admiral Grace Hopper, the creator of COBOL, an early programming language which led the way to our present-day data processing capability, is credited with saying, "You manage a filing cabinet; you lead people." That means we manage things like our automobile maintenance schedule, nuclear power plants, and our children's diets. The word *management* should be stricken from our vocabulary in any context involving people. Managers manage things and leaders lead people.

To get people to do what they will not do, or cannot do, without a leader, the leader must do the right thing. Doing the right thing is not the same as doing things right. Doing things right is when we correctly manage things. But doing the right thing involves ethics, morality, vision, and relational dynamics. To coordinate group ethics, morality, vision, and relational dynamics requires a person to be well grounded in their understanding of those things as well as possess an unusual type of courage. Effective leaders are people with a special combination of attributes. Arguments run rampant about whether leaders are born or made. Whatever the answer to that argument, it is true that one cannot be an effective leader without this special combination of personality traits, skills, and developed behavior.

Most prevailing opinions believe that the ability of people to lead others conforms roughly to Pareto's Principle or The Vital Few. Applied here, that means that about ten percent of a random population has natural leadership talents and, given the chance, will take charge of an uncontrolled situation, set goals for the group, and move the group toward those goals. Another ten percent of that population can be taught to lead, if given the proper training, and will become effective leaders. The remaining eighty percent will always be followers.

Effective leadership has certain definable characteristics. It requires a vision of excellence and an unwavering commitment to that vision. Effective leadership will not allow the group to achieve mediocrity. Leadership is about winning. We can't win all the time, but leadership *intends* to win all the time. Leadership takes people where they could never go if left to their own devices. It requires the ability to make decisions and execute changes that bring the people you lead closer to your vision. True leadership does not accept a static environment. True leadership embraces change as a constant.

Leadership requires that you be accountable for the people in your charge. Leadership is about loving those who follow you—yes, loving them with a sacrificial love. It requires that you put yourself at your people's service and serve them to meet their needs—not just tell them to buck up and deal with it (Matthew 20:25–28). It's about providing your people with what they need to get the job done. Leadership is not about turning your people loose to pursue whatever they think is right—that's abdication of leadership. Leadership identifies the strengths of each individual. When the strengths are identified, an effective leader extracts and coalesces those strengths to accomplishing the vision.

Leadership requires the type of courage to stand alone and, if necessary, sacrifice yourself for your people. This is not the inspirational burst of courage required in time of great danger—most people have that. This courage gives you the ability to stay steady, eyes forward, your people looking at your back, never wavering from your vision, no matter what may be going on around you. It's about understanding, embracing, and mastering your fear. Everyone has fear. To be sure, fear happens when bullets are flying. But real fear happens when you know bullets will be flying sometime soon and you may be out in front when it happens (Matthew 5:11–12). This type of courage will inspire the people who follow you by having them see you standing firm in times of difficulty.

Colin Powell, General (ret), U.S. Army, profiles effective leadership this way in *A Leadership Primer:*

1. Being responsible sometimes means [making people angry].
2. The day soldiers stop bringing you their problems is the day you have stopped leading them. They have either lost confidence that you can help them or concluded that you do not care.
3. Don't be buffaloed by experts and elites. Experts often [rely on their own] judgment. Elites can become so inbred that they produce hemophiliacs who bleed to death as soon as they are nicked by the real world.
4. Don't be afraid to challenge the pros, even in their own backyard.
5. Never neglect details. When everyone's mind is dulled or distracted the leader must be doubly vigilant.
6. You don't know what you can get away with until you try.
7. Keep looking below surface appearances. Don't shrink from doing so because you might not like what you find.

8. Organization doesn't really accomplish anything. Plans don't accomplish anything. Theories of management don't much matter. Endeavors succeed or fail because of the people involved. Only by attracting the best people will you accomplish great deeds.
9. Organization charts and fancy titles count for next to nothing.
10. Never let your ego get so close to your position that when your position goes, your ego goes with it.
11. Fit no stereotypes. Don't chase the latest management fads. The situation dictates which approach best accomplishes the team's mission.
12. Perpetual optimism is a force multiplier.
13. Powell's Rules for Picking People: Look for intelligence and judgment, and most critically, a capacity to anticipate, to see around corners. Also look for loyalty, integrity, a high energy drive, a balanced ego, and the drive to get things done.
14. Great leaders are almost always great simplifiers, who can cut through argument, debate, and doubt, to offer a solution everybody can understand.
15. The commander in the field is always right and the rear echelon is wrong, unless proved otherwise.
16. Have fun in your command. Don't always run at a breakneck pace. Take leave when you've earned it; spend time with your families; surround yourself with people who take their work seriously, but not themselves; those who work hard play hard.
17. Command is lonely.

Are you a leader? Being in charge doesn't make you a leader. Neither technical experience nor education equates to leadership; if they do, it is purely by happenstance. If you find yourself in a leadership role, but lack the requisite attributes of leadership, you will do a great disservice to those whom you lead. At worst you will do damage; at best you will be ineffective. The flip side is this. If you are a leader, but not occupying a leadership role, your God-given strategic talents and spiritual gifts will be wasted (Romans 12:8).

If you find yourself leading a group of Christians, or if you aspire to do so, take the following short leadership quiz. It's to be taken on your honor, meaning, no one is watching. But wait—Someone *is* watching. You can deceive yourself but you can't deceive Him. So you might as well be honest about your answers. The first ten questions examine your personality attributes and the second ten questions point to what you must do with your personality attributes.

1. Do you want to be a leader?
2. Do you have a vision of excellence?

3. Do you understand the difference between doing the right thing and doing things right?
4. Do you have a biblical worldview?
5. Do you know how to follow?
6. Do you have a deep affection for the people you are leading?
7. Do you have the courage to stand on principle?
8. Do you have the ability to make decisions?
9. Do you have the ability to execute your decisions?
10. Do you have the courage to stand alone?
11. Will you challenge the experts?
12. Will you take a risk to improve what you're doing?
13. Will you look beneath the surface and see the whole?
14. Will you put yourself last and those whom you are leading first?
15. Will you maintain optimism in the face of adversity?
16. Will you listen to complaints and accept criticism?
17. Will you make things simple for the people whom you are leading?
18. Will you trust your instincts when confirmed by Scripture?
19. Will you execute in your area of accountability regardless of what's happening elsewhere?
20. Will you have fun with your people?

If you answered "No" to any of these questions you should do some serious introspection and examine your talents, gifts, and motivations on the subject of leadership. You may be a leader or you may not be a leader. In some cases, you may be a leader but in need of more seasoning and spiritual growth before you are ready to lead. If you don't have the necessary leadership qualities you will not be able to lead God's church forward and achieve His vision of excellence, instilled in you, where you serve.

Kaizen

To lead God's church forward and achieve His vision of excellence where we serve, we need help. Indeed, "My help comes from the LORD, who made heaven and earth" (Psalm 121:2 ESV). He uses many ways to provide us this help. One of them is through the uniquely gifted people who surround us (Proverbs 11:14; 13:10). We need to tap their individual strengths solve problems, make decisions, and implement changes.

When it comes to these three activities, leaders often migrate toward one of two ends of a continuum. On one end is decision by autocracy. This is leadership by a type of benevolent dictator who makes decisions and changes based on his or her isolated knowledge and study of a situation and where all subordinate individuals take direction from a single individual in authority. On the other end of the continuum is something that has been called a self-directed work team. This team has no active leader and is comprised of a group of specialists, each knowing his or her particular job with great intimacy and how any actions taken will affect all other members of the team. Both models can work well. But they only work in very specialized circumstances.

The top-down autocratic method works well in situations of extreme stress or danger where we don't have time to adequately study, gather information, and seek input from our team. The self-directed work team works well in situations representing an assemblage of highly specialized and repeatable roles. Neither of these situations represent the majority of the circumstances in which we find ourselves anywhere in life, including the church, on a daily basis. If we try to apply the autocratic decision-making model we don't employ the collective creativity and energy of the people who surround us. If we try to apply the self-directed work team model it deteriorates into a mild form of anarchy and nothing gets done.

The traditional evangelical church uses an entirely different, third, model to be found somewhere in the middle of the continuum. The church most often uses standing committees that have a weakly defined mission, charter, timeline, or accountability focus. They are populated with people who are available rather than recruited for specific skills or knowledge. In many churches, information is maintained within a select decision-making oligarchy, and the people who can actually get things done are neither informed nor empowered to do anything. This leadership model panders to a select few with the right of eminent domain granted them for having been sitting in the same pews for several generations.

Lean requires a much different approach to problem solving—it requires *kaizen*. *Kaizen* takes the middle ground and incorporates the best elements of all three models. *Kaizen* acknowledges that leaders lead and followers follow. But it also acknowledges that there is a dynamic interdependence woven into the fabric of all roles in the organization, including all leaders and all followers. No individual has all the answers. But, taken in total, the organization *does* have all the answers; a part of each answer being resident in each individual.

As we have said, decision making, problem solving, and implementing change are rightly vested as the domain of the organization's leadership. The details of how to make decisions that eliminate waste, moving the organization forward and closer to the vision of excellence, is the domain of the people who either do the work or receive the product of the work—or both. In short, if we want to know what to do, we must simply ask the people we are leading if we are doing a good job or what we need to change to do a good job.

As we have also said, *kaizen* is a Japanese word meaning "…small change for the better." It is accomplished by "…seeking the wisdom of ten rather than the knowledge of one." So, unless we search out that wisdom and incorporate the rank and file into the decision-making process we will have little probability of making the right decision. *Kaizen* is central to an organization employing Lean principles in pursuit of continuous improvement. Many books have been written on the subject of *kaizen*. All say that Lean is impossible without it.

We have already gone into detail about much of what remains in this chapter, but some of it bears mentioning again in a few summary paragraphs.

Lean uses a lot of one- or two-word descriptors, behind each of which is a wealth of meaning. Three of them are key.

1. *Go See.* We have to go to where the work is done. This could be either a physical place such as the church or the venue in which the church is located, or it could be a metaphysical place such as the Bible—most likely both. It means we have to see the problem with our own eyes. We can't just know about the problem—we have to actually see what is working or what isn't working. We have to go and be with the people who are being affected by the problems and who know how to solve the problems. The itinerant nature of Jesus' ministry was classic "go see." He truly knew the problems of humanity because He became one of us (John 1:1–14) and He ministered among the people, not only in the Temple.

2. *Ask Why.* We need to ask the seemingly innocuous question, "Why is this happening?" This is very sensitive ground and should be approached with utmost caution. There are two ways to ask this simple question. The first, and worst, is, "Why is this happening?! Why don't you know better?! Any bonehead knows this won't work! You need to shape up and get your act together—this is important stuff we're doing!" Of course, we don't actually use those words. But, depending on how we ask the question, the listener may hear those words and we have lost the valuable input that we seek. If we do it this way, it will be a long time before he or she risks vulnerability again.

The second, and best, way to ask the question is something like, "You know, this process isn't generating the results that we were hoping for. You are a capable and devoted teacher/preacher/secretary/missionary/ administrator and it surely isn't your fault. I wonder if we could sit down and look a little deeper into the issue and see if there isn't some way we can make this both easier for you and more effective for the church?"

In both cases we've asked the simple question about why this is happening, but with the second approach our demeanor, body language, and tone result in trust rather than self-defense. The effective leader, having a good grasp on the relational dynamics required, seeks to ask the second way.

3. ***Show Respect.*** The third condition is that we must show respect for the people mired in the problem—and from whom we need to get valuable information in order to solve the problem. We can employ all the user-friendly body language, tone of voice, and suave demeanor we learned in all those self-development books and it won't make a bit of difference to the listener if we fail to show respect. We cannot fake it. Feigned respect is both condescending and patronizing. It is an insult to the listener. The listener *always* knows the difference between feigned and genuine respect.

Kaizen is about small changes, strung end-to-end, resulting in large improvements. *Kaizen* doesn't seek to write a five-year strategic plan. Rather, *kaizen* is the grist that successfully executes a five-year strategic plan. It is collaboration between all members of the organization, leaders and followers, to achieve the vision. But *kaizen* doesn't use all members at once and it doesn't proceed in a vacuum of control. It uses teams that work within established guidelines, with clear expectations and defined accountability and limited empowerment. Often, many *kaizen* teams are used at the same time, each team gathering information and making recommendations to resolve problems in different areas. A healthy *kaizen* culture of continuous improvement embraces the reality that people who do the work are then the ones to go to when problems arise. It does not rely on leadership existing in a rarified atmosphere to solve problems for them. Acts 6:1–4 models this behavior where the elders appointed deacons who had tasks to perform, but left the "how to" up to the group. Even though there were accusations of favoritism, the Hebraic widows were selected over Hellenstic widows as subject matter experts because the seven selected were steeped in the local situation and were ideal for solving the problem. A wise *kaizen* team.

Kaizen teams come in two forms, and both are drawn from the place where the work is performed—no matter whether that work is at a high or a low level.

1. **Point *Kaizen*.** These teams are more tactical in nature and tend to look at local improvements in the way that the work is done. Examples in a church include: how we collect the offering, how we keep track of children, and traffic patterns in the parking lot.

2. **Flow *Kaizen*.** Flow *kaizen* teams are more strategic in their focus and tend to have a broader view of the value stream as a whole. Flow *kaizen* teams are most interested in eliminating waste that inhibits the process of transformation in individual disciples.

In a church, a Lean ministry flow *kaizen* team would look at how the transformation process proceeds. It would examine processes used by the church to see if the disciples' needs are being ministered to and where those disciples are on their individual spiritual timelines. They would examine if the church has spurious programs that consume inordinate amounts of people resources in the form of motion, movement, time, and money that do not contribute directly to the transformation process. They would ask if there is a working process in place for assessing the spiritual gifts inventory of the congregation and then employing those spiritual gifts.

Each team has a team leader and is populated by thoughtfully selected experts. The smaller the team, the better—In the interest of eliminating waste, there is no reason to waste anyone's time by having more people than we need to deal with the problem. The team members must be selected as those who can either give, or get, the information required by the leadership to make the proper decisions.

Kaizen teams have a written charter containing a problem statement. The charter states, simply but to the point, why the team was convened. The charter also states the expected outcomes, but doesn't state the answer the team is expected to get. If the charter states that the team is expected to design and build a better mousetrap, it doesn't say that the mousetrap must be of a certain size, color, or shape. The expected outcome is that the new and improved mousetrap should kill mice more efficiently than the old one. How the team does that is up to them; this is their turf. To accomplish this goal we need to select the right people—people who know about mousetraps and killing mice.

The team must have a process owner. The process owner is the recipient of the team's product and the primary decision maker as to whether he or she will accept the product. The team also has a champion whose role it is to empower the team. The champion empowers the team by removing obstacles to their success and delegating authority downward to a practical level.

Every problem has a counterbalance. As we've discussed earlier, counterbalance is anything which the team can't compromise in the pursuit of resolving a given problem. Counterbalances are the things that are sacrosanct and can't be touched. To serve its purpose, the team must know what is within the scope of the project and what is without the scope of the project.

The team must have a timeline and an accountability focus. The team cannot be a standing committee that meets in perpetuity. The team has to have a due date for its product—a due date based in reality. The team must account for its actions and activities, generally to the champion and process owner, on a regular basis.

Kaizen teams resolve problems, put solutions in place, and move forward to the next challenge. *Kaizen* is not about the things we do well—*kaizen* is about the things that get in the way of what we do well.

Kaizen works anywhere—it will work in the church if we are willing to risk vulnerability and transparency as Jesus did. It is leadership's role to set goals, remove barriers, and provide a vision of excellence. It is leadership's role to define the team's mission and establish guiding principles for their activity. Leadership provides the "what" and the *kaizen* teams provide the "how." It would be tragic to face God and realize that we held a vision that brought Him to our level rather than us to His.

HIGHLAND COMMUNITY CHURCH—Wausau, WI
A Lean Analysis of Our Ministry

In December of 2009 I was asked to contribute to the book you are now reading. I was just a little bit confused as to how I help with something about which I knew nothing. Barely sidestepping cynicism, I remained skeptical that this was yet another attempt by someone to remake the church in his image or to run a church like a business—two efforts that have most times proved troublesome. But, since my role was to ensure scriptural correctness and connectivity to the subject, I agreed. Along the way I learned a lot about Lean and how it can work in any organization, including churches and church plants.

During the development of the book we performed an analysis of Highland's core ministry programs and their effectiveness and efficiency at providing what we hoped was value for God—His glory through transformation of individual lives. If we were going to write this book we needed to know if the shoemaker's kids actually *did* have shoes. To do this we had to assign empirical values, and measureable qualities and quantities, to elements of our spiritual lives and our ministries that have always been treated as ephemeral, conceptual, abstract, and beyond the pale of human definition. In short, to our knowledge, an analysis like this had never been done in a ministry environment before. And we had to be completely unafraid, unemotional, and impartial—a tall order in a historically successful urban church of about 2,000 people.

We used some classic Lean tools to define what it is that we do at Highland and what it is that we hope to achieve at Highland. We defined our people groups; we distilled elements of spiritual DNA common to all believers; we defined everything we do at Highland in terms of waste and value when compared to God's definition of value.

The results were illuminating, to say the least—you can read a full description of the analysis and its findings in Appendix B of this book. In summary, we learned:

- Some of the programs were performing as we expected. Our youth programs are very effective at reaching young lives as well as consuming little financial and human resources.
- Some of the programs were falling short. Sunday school consumes an inordinate amount of our resources, both human and financial, and achieves little impact on people's lives. But to eliminate it at this time would be too traumatic to the church. We will silently let it move itself into the background while we devote ourselves to more effective and efficient programs. We found that we expect too much out of the Sunday service in its present conformation, and we will strengthen it by more directly connecting it to our small group ministries.
- Some ministries were performing better than we thought. Our small group ministry is very effective and also consumes very few of our resources, as do our short-term missions programs. We found that those more successful programs did, in fact, use the Lean continuous improvement principle of kaizen—although we didn't know it by that name.

We learned that we do some things right and that some things need improvement. The analysis gave us a baseline of where to begin a structured continuous improvement process and minimize or eliminate that which consumes much and produces little.

– Dr. Jeffrey Hinds, Senior Pastor
Highland Community Church, Wausau, WI

Chapter 9

Accountability for Our Lives

"There must be some kind of way out of here
Said the joker to the thief.
There's too much confusion
I can't get no relief."

"All Along the Watchtower"
— Bob Dylan, 1967

A book on implementing change would not be complete without a discussion of accountability, and it seems fitting to close with that subject. Christianity is very much about accountability (Galatians 6:1–2), but it is a subject that doesn't get enough attention in the contemporary evangelical church.

These are the facts: our sin has separated us from God (Romans 6:23). We are incapable, in our own power, to restore the relationship that has been broken (Ephesians 2:8–9). We broke our relationship with God through sin (Romans 5:10–21), and we continue to break it every day. God did not do it to us. We did it to ourselves. God's desire is to reconcile us back to Him. God, through the sinless sacrifice of Himself, in the Second Person of the Trinity, Jesus Christ, died for us to restore our relationship with Him (John 3:16; 14:1–6; Titus 3:4–6). Jesus was wrongly accused, tried by a kangaroo court, and lynched in a most humiliating and barbaric way—all for us (Matthew 26–28). Then on the cross, all of our sins were heaped on Christ because the wages of our sin is death and Jesus willingly sacrificed Himself for our sins (Romans 6:23; 2 Corinthians 5:21). He died so that through faith in Him alone, we might be forgiven, cleansed, and redeemed forever. In so doing He defined the timeless essence of accountability.

Have you placed your faith in Christ alone, His death, burial, and resurrection as the sole payment for your confessed sins, and in the power of His Spirit, have you asked God to help you repent and turn from your sins and to grant you everlasting life? If the Bible is to be believed, this is the only way to become a child of God. If you have not already, won't you, by faith, receive Christ as your personal Savior?

If you accept these facts as undisputed, that acceptance predicates some undisputable conclusions as to how we account to God for what He has done for us. And that accountability must take some practical form as we live out our lives. We cannot repay Christ for sacrificing Himself so that we might be forgiven and granted eternal life, yet every action of our temporal existence should be an action of accountability that brings glory to Him. Not accountability resulting from fear but from gratitude—and from love, that most basic attribute of God that served to initiate this sequence of events we call Christianity. Even though we have been forgiven our sins, past, present, and future, we will account to Him and be judged for the stewardship of what we have been given while here on earth (2 Corinthians 5:10; 1 Corinthians 3:10–15). Believers will never face condemnation because Jesus took the condemnation for us on the cross (Romans 8:1), but we will give an accounting for how we used our time, resources, and lives for His great purposes.

God is not accountable to us, but He is accountable to His own nature and His perfect plan. He has set in motion a plan that is hardwired to His very nature and He will not violate it. He has made promises to us. He has made Himself accountable not to break those promises and to reward us even though we have done nothing to deserve it. He will not break His promises or violate what He has set in motion—to do so would be to violate Himself.

This accountability between Him and us is the model upon which all of our behaviors and relationships are judged as right and wrong, true and untrue, valuable or valueless. It is we who are flawed and often fail in our accountability to Him. It is He who is perfect and never fails us. Because of this, we embrace a system and standard of behavior that is as different from our natural inclinations as the builder of a house is different from the house he has built. We must never compromise the standard of accountability even though we exhibit compromising behaviors every day.

Accountability is a tough word that conjures up tough images with maybe a bit of fear and trembling involved. The root word for accountability is the word "account." To account means to answer to a higher authority for our role in an event or a sequence of events over which we have control or for which we have been charged. As such, success or failure is implied. Success is good and failure is not good. Is it any wonder that we avoid dealing with it? But it shouldn't have to be that way. God has promised never to ask more of us than for what we are able to answer. Yes, it may be difficult at times. But never more than we can accomplish.

By contrast, responsibility is easy to understand and not uncomfortable to digest. Responsibility's root word is "response." Response means to take some kind of action based on the expectations of someone or something. Responsibility refers to jobs; it refers to things that people do. To be responsible is to execute a task or sequence of tasks. Responsibility is a duty or obligation that requires we put our hands on something and take some action. Thus far the book has primarily dealt with the subject of responsibility, meaning, what are we going to do with what we've been given? To bring closure to the book, it's time to ask the questions, "Why do we have to do anything with what we've been given? What is the attribute of our lives that demands accountability? What characteristic of our existence is important enough for God to ask us to answer for our actions now that we've been saved?" The answer to these questions is simple and harks back to the start of the book. We answer to God Himself because we are the stewards of His glory, and His glory is manifest in the actions we take. We must answer for them.

Even though accountability and responsibility are different words, and have different meanings, the two go hand-in-hand. One can't answer for something that one hasn't been asked to account for; and one can't be asked to do something for which one doesn't have to answer.

To understand the model of accountability provided by God Himself and how He values it, and so that we may use that model to minister to the people He loves, we must understand our position inside a three-dimensional model of spiritual accountability, shown below. The X-axis is horizontal; the Y-axis is vertical; the Z-axis is coming out of the paper toward you.

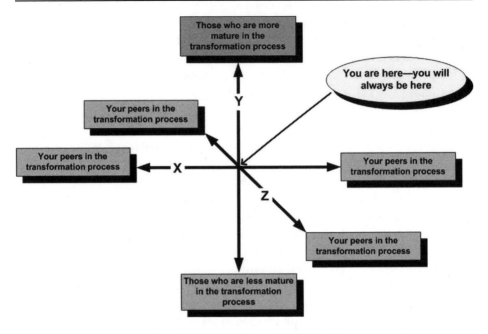

Figure 9.1: Spiritual Accountability Model

No matter where we are in the transformation process we will always find ourselves at the intersection of these three axes. The X-axis and the Z-axis represent the spiritual plane on which we find ourselves. This is the place where we will always be no matter if we become great or small; no matter if we become mature in Christ or we stay as a child.

The X-axis and Z-axis represent our relationship to all the people with whom we are peers in the transformation process. These are the people with whom we are more or less at the same point on God's *takt* timeline of transformation. We are accountable to these people to bear them up. We are accountable to share what we have learned as well as to learn from them. We are accountable to not provide stumbling blocks to their development. We are accountable to fellowship with them and they with us. We are accountable to labor with them side-by-side executing our responsibilities, as God has given them to us.

The Y-axis represents two other groups of people. The first group is those believers who have progressed further along in the transformation process than have we. They occupy the area on the Y-axis above the intersection point. We are accountable to be led by these people. We are accountable to submit to mentoring by these people. We are accountable to show them the respect they deserve as having been brought further along in their journey than we. It is from the group above the intersection point that our leaders should be drawn.

The second group on the Y-axis is that group of believers who are less mature than we are in the transformation process. They occupy the area on the X-axis from the intersection point downward. We are accountable to mentor these people as God brings them across our paths. We are accountable to nurture them as a mother nurtures a newborn baby. We are accountable to serve as a model for these people. We are accountable to not judge these people as being inferior Christians even if they are less mature than we. This area of the model includes those who have not yet been called to redemption through Jesus Christ.

As we mature in Christ we will move up the Y-axis of the model. But no matter where we are in the transformation process, we will always find ourselves at some 3-axis intersection, representing our relationship to three separate broadly defined groups of people. This model represents our relationship to believers and unbelievers alike. There will always be people less mature to support and for whom to set an example, including those who do not yet believe. There will always be a peer group to labor with side-by-side. And there will always be a group who is more mature to emulate and support as they imitate Christ.

Finally, above all of us, no matter where we find ourselves in this model, is God— to whom we are all accountable to use wisely all we have or ever will have. We believe that Lean is an excellent tool to help us in our accountability to God. Lean enables us to minimize the seven deadly wastes of the twenty-first-century church by using God's resources for His greatest glory.

Soli Deo Gloria—For the Glory of God Alone.

EPILOGUE

May God bless and keep you always,
May your wishes all come true,
May you always do for others
And let others do for you.
May you build a ladder to the stars
And climb on every rung,
May you stay forever young,
Forever young, forever young,
May you stay forever young.

May you grow up to be righteous,
May you grow up to be true,
May you always know the truth
And see the lights surrounding you.
May you always be courageous,

Stand upright and be strong,
May you stay forever young,
Forever young, forever young,
May you stay forever young.

May your hands always be busy,
May your feet always be swift,
May you have a strong foundation
When the winds of changes shift.
May your heart always be joyful,
May your song always be sung,
May you stay forever young,
Forever young, forever young,
May you stay forever young.

"Forever Young"
Bob Dylan, 1973

A Lean Ministry Lexicon

Accountability
The state of being accountable; liable to be called on to render an account for a task or sequence of tasks. Normally connotes decision-making authority.

Batch Processing
Producing more than one piece of an item and moving those items to the next operation before they are actually needed. A batch of parts is put through Process A and set aside. They are then moved to the next area where Process B is performed on the entire batch before they move again. The parts then wait in another queue for the next process. After a while they are shifted to another area where Process C is performed. This batch-and-queue process is continued until the entire batch of parts is completed.

Believer
Anyone having confessed their sins and accepted forgiveness and salvation through the sinless sacrifice of Jesus Christ as the only Son of God; and, someone having made a personal commitment to Jesus Christ of an enduring nature; and, someone who believes that, because of this acceptance, he or she will spend eternity in Heaven in the company of other believers with Almighty God.

Biblical worldview
Per the Barna Group, a person with a biblical worldview believes eight things:
- Jesus Christ lived a sinless life.
- God is the all-powerful and all-knowing Creator of the universe and He still rules it today.
- Salvation is a gift from God and cannot be earned.
- Satan is real.
- A Christian has a responsibility to share his or her faith in Christ with other people.

- The Bible is accurate in all of the principles it teaches.
- Unchanging moral truth exists.
- Such truth is defined by the Bible.

Change agent
A [Lean] change agent is someone who will lead the organization from traditional behaviors to becoming a Lean organization; the architect of a change initiative. This person may come from within or from outside the organization.

Church
"*The* church" refers to the Bride of Christ or the church-at-large. "A church" refers to any group of believers gathered into a local congregation.

Continuous improvement
The ongoing process or philosophy of doing things better, faster, and cheaper; but implies more than improvement in basic processes. It describes a philosophy whereby an organization and the individuals within it undertake continual improvements of all aspects of organizational performance, striving for perfection by continually removing successive layers of waste as they are discovered and continually improving the quality of the product.

Counterbalance
A critical element of the organization that cannot be compromised by actions, activities, or improvements executed elsewhere in the organization.

Customer
The person or people who establish quality and quantity expectation and set the demand schedule for any and all products, goods, and services; the end-user of the product; the recipient of the product; the reason for the existence of any organization.

Enlightenment/Enlightenment Project
This describes the work of thinkers such as Francis Bacon, René Descartes, and Isaac Newton, among others, which led to the elevation of the human thinking self to be the center of reality and pictured the physical world as a machine whose laws and regularity could be discerned by the human mind. Under the banner of the Enlightenment Project, philosophers and scientists sought to unlock the secrets of the universe in order to master nature for human benefit and create a better world. This quest led to the modern technological society characteristic of the twentieth century with its attempt to employ rational management to improve the quality of life. Enlightenment thinking accepts that knowledge is

certain, objective, and inherently good and embraces some form of unified, all-encompassing, and universally valid explanation, including a Metanarrative story of mankind.

Flow
In its purest form continuous flow means that items are processed and moved immediately to the next process one piece at a time; each processing step completes its work just before the next process needs the item, and the transfer batch is one piece. Also known as "one-piece flow" and "make-one, move-one."

Follower
Someone who demonstrates allegiance to a person, a doctrine, a cause, and the like, generally based on a personal relationship and a regard for a person's ideas or belief; a servant, subordinate, disciple, or adherent who subscribes to the teachings or methods of another.

Kaizen
The Japanese word for continuous improvement through incremental changes; implies more than improvement in basic processes. *Kaizen* represents a philosophy whereby an organization and the individuals within it undertake continual improvements of all aspects of organizational life; as the name implies, continuous improvement never ends; all improvements can be further improved.

Leader
Any person who leads; a guiding or directing head of any organized group or movement; one who goes before to show the way; one who influences or induces; one who guides in vision, direction, course, action, and opinion; a visionary.

Lean Enterprise or Lean
Originally known as Lean Manufacturing, Lean Enterprise is a broader application of Lean principles to health care and service businesses as well as manufacturing.

Lean Manufacturing
Originally known as the Toyota Production System; a manufacturing environment embracing a culture of continuous improvement targeting the elimination of seven categories of waste.

Non-Value-Added
Any activities or actions that add no real value to the product or service; such activities or actions are considered a form of waste.

Postmodern, postmodernism, or postmodernity
An intellectual shift that questions, and even rejects, the Enlightenment Project and the foundational assumptions upon which it was built (See *Enlightenment/ Enlightenment Project*). Postmodernism marks the end of a single worldview. It resists unified, all-encompassing, universally valid explanations such as the biblical Metanarrative of mankind. It replaces these with a respect for difference and a celebration of the local and particular at the expense of the universal. Postmodernism likewise entails a rejection of the emphasis on rational discovery through the scientific method which provided the intellectual foundation for the modern attempt to construct a better world. This radically distances the postmodern individual from modern philosophies about truth and knowledge.

Pull
Pull exists when demand for goods and services is exerted from the end-user; to produce or process an item only when the customer needs it and has requested it—the customer can be internal or external; in a pull system no one upstream should produce goods or services until the customer downstream requires it.

Push
To produce or process an item without any real demand from the customer, creating inventory and all other forms of waste.

Responsibility
A duty or obligation requiring a response from someone; taking some kind of action based on direction from higher authority.

Spiritual DNA
Eight elements of spirituality characterizing the desires and needs resident in all believers past, present, and future. These occur at the most basic level and represent a DNA structure that identifies us as all belonging to the same spiritual gene pool. These are:
- Education
- Evangelism and Missions
- Fellowship
- Prayer
- Service/Compassion
- Stewardship
- Wisdom
- Worship

Steward/Stewardship
One who does not own but manages another's property or other critical affairs; one who administers anything as the agent of another or others, includes managing, buying, obtaining, directing, etc; implies subordination to and working at the direction of higher authority.

Sub-optimization
A condition where gains made in one activity are offset by equal or greater losses in another activity.

Takt
The German word for pace or rhythm; the rate of demand from the customer. It is used in Lean to match the rate of production to the rate of customer demand.

Toyota Production System (TPS)
The manufacturing strategy of Toyota developed after World War II, regarded as the first implementation of Lean Manufacturing.

Transformation Process
A four-stage process transforming the eight elements of spiritual DNA characteristic to every believer, beginning at the moment of conversion and continuing for the life of the believer. These stages were characterized in Bill Hull's book *Jesus Christ, Disciplemaker*. The stages are:
1. Come and See: Our initial discovery of the King and His Kingdom
2. Come and Follow Me: Formed to live a kingdom life
3. Come and Be with Me: Equipped to harvest for the kingdom
4. Go and Make Disciples: Sent to harvest for the kingdom

Value
Attributes and features of a product or service that are worth paying for in the eyes of customers; what does and does not create value is to be specified from the customer's perspective and not from the perspective of individual companies, functions, or departments; a product or service provided to a customer at the right time, at an appropriate price, as defined in each case by the customer.

Value-Added
Any action or activity that incrementally changes something from one state into another; activities or work that is essential to ensure a product or service meets the needs of the customer; activities or actions taken that add real value to the product or service; any activity that is not waste.

Value Stream

A chain of value-creating processes; all the things done to create value for the customer; all activities required to bring a product or service to the hands of the customer.

Value Stream Map

A Lean planning tool used to visualize the value stream of a process, department, or organization. Value stream mapping is a systematic method to identify all the activities required to produce a product or product family; first drawn to show the current state and then redrawn to show the future state.

Waste

Any activity absorbing resources that creates no real value for the customer; anything that does not add value to the product or service; an activity the customer wouldn't want to pay for if they knew it was happening. Lean theory categorizes waste as:

1. Defects
2. Excessive transportation
3. Inappropriate processing
4. Overproduction
5. Unnecessary inventory
6. Unnecessary motion
7. Waiting

Appendix B

Lean Analysis:
Highland Community Church – Wausau, WI

Executive Summary

In January through May of 2010, Highland Community Church (HCC) of Wausau, Wisconsin, conducted a baseline Lean analysis of the church's programs and their ability to effectively and efficiently function as organs of transformation for the congregation. The analysis both qualified and quantified the impact of those programs and defined strengths, weaknesses, and opportunities for improvement. The analysis was led by Dr. Jeffrey Hinds, Senior Pastor, with the assistance of Charles Duffert, an experienced Lean practitioner and advisor.

The analysis used empirical methods to quantify and qualify what is normally considered intangible and conceptual. Gathering this data was, and will continue to be, important to HCC. Churches, and church leaders, who fear data are often avoiding disturbing trends. None of us enjoy facing our shortfalls and learning that what we are doing is wasteful and ineffective. Yet unless we use data, we can only rely on anecdotal or tribal knowledge, making it difficult to initiate improvement. Tribal knowledge is useful within its context, but it does not help identify waste or objectively determine where transformation occurs or does not occur. Church leaders must impartially and unemotionally face these truths to examine which areas of their ministry are most effectively glorifying God and transforming people into His likeness. Then we can place our most effective people, and the bulk of our resources, where we are effective because God is moving in those areas.

After the relevant data is gathered, changes must be executed in an environment sensitive to the historical culture of a church or organization. The older the church, the more important it becomes to know and to honor the culture of that church's history. New church plants can make changes on a dime, while one-hundred-year-old organizations turn more slowly than battleships. Stringently using data alone, without concern for the historical culture of an organization, can lead to unnecessary unrest or even destruction.

A broad-brush summary of findings ranked HCC's primary programs from most- to least-effective on the transformation of the spiritual DNA of the individual attender as:

Rank	Program Name	Percent of Potential Impact
1.	Generation 180 (youth program)	51.6%
2.	Connection Care Groups (small groups)	48.4%
3.	Short-term missions trip programs	41.2%
4.	Sunday service	34.6%
5.	Leadership Highland (training for leadership at HCC)	25.9%
6.	Singles ministries (two different groups)	17.2%
7.	Sunday school/adult Bible fellowships	16.1%
8.	Women's Bible studies	15.9%
9.	One-Way Clubs (children's program)	12.4%

As ineffective as the data shows adult Sunday school to be, HCC has a culture and history of well-attended Sunday schools and it would be unwise to simply shut them down. It would be too traumatic for the church. HCC has hundreds of adults, generally longer-term Highlanders, attending Sunday school. Yet all evidence indicates that its small group ministry (CCGs) is far more effective for both newer and longer-term attenders.

To eliminate Sunday school outright would be to alienate the longest attending, and most invested, core constituency. However, the data encourages HCC to focus more resources into small group ministries rather than adult Sunday school classes and respond to Sunday school with less staff effort. HCC will continue to staff and advertise adult Sunday school, but this program will be considered less core than it has been. Simultaneously, HCC will maximize efforts towards small groups, as these are clearly the preferred discipleship model of newer (and many older) attenders, as well as better at glorifying God through a more effective transformation process.

Findings also show HCC gets the most "bang for its buck" out of the Generation 180 youth program. Tribal knowledge had indicated this but now the data confirms it. Focusing on Generation 180 will help HCC determine future staffing needs and prepare new leaders for the twenty-first-century church. To ensure cost-effectiveness, the church will use more paid and volunteer staff in this vital area.

HCC's short-term missions program is one of the few programs that, by design, reaches outside the church. These missions projects are effective, efficient, and transformational. The church uses its resources well in this program to minister globally and return residual benefits back into the church to help its own participants grow and mature in Christ.

As it is in many churches, the Sunday morning service is Highland's focal point. The analysis did not examine the perceptions of the congregation-at-large regarding the Sunday service. But anecdotal evidence, including a recent church-wide survey, indicates that many people attend Highland because of these services. Repeated testimonies during new member interviews, the ten-week orientation class for prospective members, and newcomer receptions also indicate that this may be true. If so, it indicates a significant strength. However, it may also be true that public affection for the Sunday service is due to Jeff Hinds' exceptional exegetical preaching and teaching on Sunday morning. If this is true, it indicates a weakness in that the church expects to accomplish unrealistic goals in a seventy-five-minute period on Sundays.

Though this is the first hard data analysis to be performed at HCC, it is by no means the only analysis. The church conducts approximately 150 soft data interviews with about 60% of the congregation pointing to Sunday worship services and sermons as the main reason for attendance. There is an inherent risk in this method in that the interviewee often does not tell the truth, the whole truth, and nothing but the truth to the interviewer for fear of offense. Also, these interviews do not assess the level of spiritual transformation actually occurring during these services. This analysis affirms that there is a lot of room for improvement in this area. Our findings show that linking the small group ministry to the Sunday sermon more strongly will significantly strengthen both programs. This is presently being addressed by transitioning HCC small groups into sermon-based small groups to discuss and further apply the Sunday morning messages.

This analysis produced a great number of charts, graphs, spreadsheets, and tables. To include them here would only serve to confuse the reader. Most of them have been omitted for the sake of brevity and clarity. Our summarized findings appear below.

HCC Profile

HCC is well established in this 60,000-person community of the Upper Wisconsin River Valley. It is elder-directed, staff-led, but the congregation has ultimate authority in all matters. The church has a large congregation and considers itself to be first a teaching center with other supporting programs, and is led by a gifted teacher in the person of its senior pastor, Dr. Jeffrey Hinds. The church employs fifteen full-time-equivalents, including 7 pastors, and uses 600+ unpaid, volunteer, and intermittent staff per month to administer its programs.

HCC states its mission as: *Seeking to glorify God by helping people take the next step in their relationship to Jesus Christ.*

The congregation is comprised of 73% families and 27% singles, with the median age being approximately 40 years. The gender mix is almost evenly split with the socioeconomic status being middle- to upper-middle class, leaning toward upper-middle. The congregation's professional status is mixed professional and para-professional, leaning toward professional. About 75% of the congregation is college-educated and greater than 90% are of European/Anglo ethnicity.

HCC People Groups

HCC has seven distinct primary people groups targeted for ministry. These are:
1. Adults
2. Children (3rd—5th graders)
3. Church Leadership
4. External People Groups
5. Singles
   a. Journeys (over 35)
   b. Young Singles (18–35)
   c. Over Fifty
6. Youth (6th–12th graders)
7. Women

HCC Transformation Programs

HCC permits and encourages any creative fellowship, worship, or teaching experience that leads to the transformation of the individual disciple. But it formally nurtures nine distinct programs. These are:

1. **Connection Care Groups:** Adult and/or family small groups (eight to twenty-five people) who are engaged in sermon-based Bible studies, fellowship, worship, congregational care, and ministry projects.
2. **Generation 180 (youth program):** Sixth- through twelfth-graders who engage in Bible studies, small groups, active events, worship bands, etc.

3. **Leadership Highland:** An invitation-only (for twenty-five to thirty-five people per year) program to develop leadership at Highland. It includes reading, class time, and homework.
4. **One-Way Clubs (children's program):** Kindergarten through fifth-graders engaging in Bible studies, small groups, active events, worship bands, etc.
5. **Short-term Missions Trip Programs:** Short- and long-term foreign missions.
6. **Singles Ministries:** A young singles adult group, a thirty to fifty age group, and an over fifty age group.
7. **Sunday School/Adult Bible Fellowships:** Age- and gender-specific classroom teaching.
8. **Sunday Service:** Preaching, teaching, music, and prayer.
9. **Women's Bible Studies:** Morning and evening Women of Real Devotion (WORD) Bible studies, MOPS, and Church Women Go (outdoor activities and fellowship).

DNA Target Focus

HCC leadership embraces the concept that transformation glorifies God and that transformation into the likeness of Jesus Christ is His primary desire. HCC leadership believes that the material being transformed within each believer is the eight elements of spiritual DNA described in this book. They weight the relative focus of HCC ministry to each of those elements as shown below.

DNA Element	Relative Focus of HCC Ministry (1-10)
Education/Learning	10
Prayer	8
Wisdom	8
Evangelism, Outreach & Missions	7
Stewardship	5
Worship	5
Fellowship	4
Service & Compassion	4

Figure B.1: DNA Target Focus

Analysis Methodology

Analysis Approach.   Following is a flow diagram showing the sequence of analysis events.

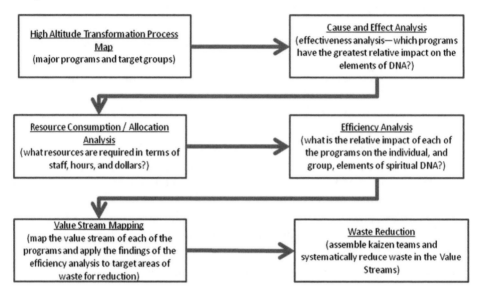

Figure B.2: HCC Analysis Sequence

Analysis Assumptions. The following assumptions were agreed to before starting the analysis.
- All believers possess the same eight elements of spiritual DNA.
- It is the believer's DNA that is incrementally changed into the likeness of Jesus Christ.
- The transformation process occurs in four distinct stages.
- All churches have waste.
- All the church's activities are either:
  - o Waste
  - o Non-waste
- Waste does not glorify or obey God.
- Waste degrades the process of transformation.
- Waste must be eliminated to effectively glorify or obey God.
- Lean eliminates waste in any process in any organization.
- HCC can use Lean to eliminate waste.

Transformation Programs Map. The following high-altitude process map shows HCC's primary transformation programs and links them to the church's people groups.

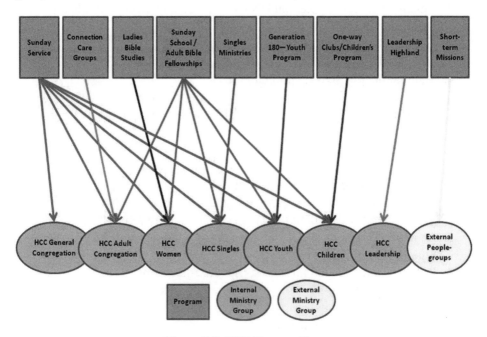

Figure B.3: HCC Process Map

Resource Categories. The following resource categories were considered when analyzing transformation program efficiency.
1. Paid staff
2. Unpaid staff
3. Volunteer staff
4. Paid staff prep time
5. Paid staff execution time
6. Unpaid staff prep time
7. Unpaid staff execution time
8. Volunteer prep time
9. Volunteer execution time
10. Utility-hours used
11. Utilities rate
12. Paid staff rate
13. Debt service

Performance Attributes. The following twenty quantitative results were reported:

1. Relative impact on overall DNA of any given individual by program type
2. Relative percent of potential DNA impact on any given individual by program type
3. Total number of paid staff by program type
4. Total number of unpaid and volunteer staff by program type
5. Total number of staff by program type
6. Total paid staff time in person-hours by program type
7. Total paid, unpaid, and volunteer staff time in person-hours by program type
8. Total prep time in person-hours by program type
9. Total execution time in person-hours by program type
10. Total paid staff cost ($) by program type
11. Total financial cost ($) by program type
12. Relative impact / total number paid staff by program type
13. Relative impact / total number unpaid and volunteer staff by program type
14. Relative impact / total number staff by program type
15. Relative impact / total paid staff in person-hours by program type
16. Relative impact / total number of paid, unpaid, and volunteer staff in person-hours by program type
17. Relative impact / total prep time in person-hours by program type
18. Relative impact / total execution in person-hours by program type
19. Relative impact / total paid staff cost ($) by program type
20. Relative impact / total financial cost ($) by program type

Findings

Conclusions and recommendations for each of the nine primary programs are summarized below.

Generation 180 Youth Groups

Conclusions: Of all nine programs at HCC, the Generation 180 youth program has the most significant overall impact on the spiritual DNA of a given member in that program, achieving 51.6% of its potential. Generation 180 is also the most efficient of all nine programs when considering total paid, unpaid, and volunteer staff human resources (although much of this resource is consumed with preparation) and total financial costs of the program. Its efficiency is primarily due to it being an almost entirely volunteer enterprise.

Recommendations: Because this group is the immediate future of HCC, and other churches, we recommend the church establish a *kaizen* team to examine ways to build upon the success of this program and to extrapolate the elements of efficiency and effectiveness to other programs needing them. The team should focus particularly on the opportunity to export the success of volunteer staff involvement and should also examine the feasibility of splitting the group into the more commonly accepted categories of Mosaics (born between 1984 and 2002) and Busters (born between 1965 and 1983).

Connection Care Groups (CCGs)

Conclusions: CCGs achieve a significant impact and are the second most overall effective program at HCC. They receive and process teaching material during the week that was introduced during the Sunday sermon. They achieve 48.4% of their potential impact on the spiritual DNA of a given participant. They are also the second most efficient program when considering the use of paid staff as well as total financial cost for the program. When considering the additional resource of unpaid and volunteer staff, CCG impact drops to moderate. When considering requirements for preparation and execution time, CCG impact drops to between moderate and little.

Recommendations: Establish a *kaizen* team to examine HCC's primary role as a teaching church and the possibility of expanding the role of CCGs in the teaching process. The team should consider slowly shifting the focus of the teaching experience from Sunday morning to weekly CCG group fellowship and actively campaign to incorporate more of the congregation into CCGs. This will encourage a shift in focus from the Sunday sermon being an information-processing experience to an information-introduction experience and will strengthen both programs individually as well as corporately. Further, the team should consider establishing a robust measurement feedback tool to empirically determine any given CCG member's:
   o Ability to process the sermon information
   o Ability to apply the sermon information
   o Feedback to the pastor for correction/improvement of the sermon information
This measurement/feedback tool should be formatted to provide a corporate, as well as individual, profile of the effectiveness of the teaching experience.

Short-Term Missions

Conclusions: Short-term missions have high to moderate impact on the spiritual DNA of a given participant, achieving 41.2% of their potential, but it is one of only a few externally focused programs of the church and touches fewer total persons than do any of the other programs. Short-term missions are very cost-effective at HCC because they use mostly unpaid and volunteer staff. It is the most financially efficient of all nine programs, considering that it uses little to no paid staff and consumes little of the church's regular financial resources. However, short-term missions are generally executed as short-term foreign missions and not to the community in which HCC resides.

Recommendations: Establish a *kaizen* team to examine the feasibility of extrapolating the effectiveness and efficiency of HCC's short-term foreign missions program to the local community.

Sunday Service

Conclusions: The Sunday service is the centerpiece of HCC's repertoire of programs. The church demands a lot out of the Sunday service, expecting it to touch six distinct people groups during an approximate seventy-five-minute period. Data shows that it achieves only moderate impact on the spiritual DNA of any given participant, or 34.6% of its potential. The Sunday service is loosely linked to the Connection Care Group program at HCC insomuch as the groups are expected to review and process Sunday sermon material during their weekly meetings. However, a minority of the congregation is active in CCGs—presently about 40% of adults and 80% of children. The Sunday service does, in fact, touch more individual lives than any of the other programs at HCC, and anecdotal evidence shows that many, if not most, of the congregation attends HCC *because* of the Sunday service. The church needs a robust measurement tool to more fully grasp the impact of the Sunday service on the collective spiritual DNA of the congregation, a need that is beyond the scope of this analysis. The service requires a significant level of human resources in terms of paid, unpaid, and volunteer staff effort to produce and execute, giving it little impact per unit of resource consumed. It is very inefficient as well as being marginally effective.

Recommendations: Maintain the Sunday service as is, even though it appears to fall short of expectation. To eliminate or significantly change the Sunday service at this time would destabilize it and the programs depending on it and would minimize HCC's strength as a teaching church. Senior Pastor Jeff Hinds' greatest strength is his ability to teach and exegete applicable spiritual truths to everyday situations in everyday people's lives. But we believe that most of the congregation sees the Sunday service as the culmination of, rather than the beginning of, weekly activities.

Establish a *kaizen* team to slowly change the focus of the Sunday service from that of an information-processing experience to an information-introduction experience by bolstering attendance and the teaching/learning/information-processing activities of the Connection Care Groups (see recommendations for CCGs, above).

Leadership Highland

Conclusions: Leadership Highland achieves a moderate impact on the spiritual DNA of any given participant, achieving 25.9% of its potential impact. Its impact is reduced to little when considering the total number of paid staff hours required for administration.

Recommendations: Continue Leadership Highland as is because it is a critical activity that should be the basis for developing Christian leaders at HCC. But, assemble a *kaizen* team to investigate ways to make the program more efficient and effective. Investigate the possibility of using alternative teaching and/or outside leadership development resources to strengthen the program.

Singles Ministry

Conclusions: Singles ministries achieve little impact on the spiritual DNA of a given member relative to the eight other programs, achieving 17.2% of their potential. They consume a disproportionate level of human resources and have moderate impact per total number of paid staff, but little impact when considering the total number of unpaid and volunteer staff. The program also consumes too many preparation and execution hours, reducing its value to little to moderate when considering those resources.

Recommendations: Establish a *kaizen* team for the purpose of reducing preparation and execution time associated with the program and reducing the present level of human resources consumption.

Sunday School/Adult Bible Fellowships

Conclusions: Analysis findings show that Sunday school/adult fellowships have little to no impact on the spiritual DNA of a given member and only achieve 16.1%

of their potential impact. As well as being ineffective, they are very inefficient. They disproportionately consume the following resources:

o Total number of paid staff
o Total number of unpaid and volunteer staff
o Total number of staff
o Total paid staff person-hours
o Total unpaid and volunteer staff person-hours
o Total preparation time
o Total execution time
o Total staff cost ($)
o Total program cost ($)

Sunday school/adult fellowships consumes:

o 70% more paid, unpaid, and volunteer staff than the next closest
o 350% more paid, unpaid, and volunteer person-hours than the next closest
o 350% more preparation and execution hours than the next closest
o High-moderate paid staff cost ($)
o Significant total program financial cost ($)

Recommendations: Establish a *kaizen* team to examine the feasibility of continuing Sunday school/adult Bible fellowships in their present configuration; to find ways to minimize the consumption of valuable human resources that could be more constructively used elsewhere; and to change the church's focus and allocation of resources to other more effective programs.

Women's Bible Studies

Conclusions: Women's Bible studies achieve little to moderate overall impact on the spiritual DNA of an individual participant, achieving 15.9% of their potential, but consume very little of the church's resources because they are administered on a near-total volunteer basis.

Recommendations: Continue as is; no change.

One-Way Clubs (children's ministries)

Conclusions: One-Way Clubs achieve the least impact of all nine programs on the spiritual DNA of a given participant, achieving only 12.4% of their potential. There is negligible to no impact on the individual participant when considering use of total staff and total financial input. This is particularly unfortunate because these children need Christian principles and education solidly inculcated during these delicate years to serve as the baseline for their journey of transformation and to fulfill God's plan for them as men and women of the developing twenty-first-century church.

Recommendations: Establish a *kaizen* team to examine a complete overhaul of children's ministries at HCC.

ACKNOWLEDGMENTS

"Oh, I get by with a little help from my friends.
Mm, gonna try with a little help from my friends.
Yes, I get by with a little help from my friends,
...with a little help from my friends."
"With a Little Help From My Friends"

– John Lennon and Paul McCartney, 1967

Writing a book is a hard thing to do. It takes a full measure of monumental stupidity and towering arrogance, combined with unbounded naiveté, to take the time and effort to write something down and expect that anyone will read it—let alone pay money to read it. A book, like pretty much everything else in life, is a group effort. A book is a group effort like giving birth is a group effort. Both are long and drawn-out experiences fraught with discomfort and anxiety. Now, mind you, neither of us has actually given birth—but we have both seen it done several times. The process is not pretty. But the hope of the creators of either type of offspring is that the result of their efforts becomes something beautiful that will enrich their lives and the lives of the people around them. This book was conceived in a tent in a remote corner of the John and Margaret Grant ranch in east central Wyoming. The book developed a heartbeat, lungs, and fingernails at Mike and Donna Ball's guesthouse at land's end in Door County, Wisconsin. The book developed internal organs and began to kick and punch at Paul and Gail Myers's wilderness retreat just south of International Falls, Minnesota. Our gratitude to all.

We would like to acknowledge the following persons as part of the group birthing effort.

Thanks to Dr. Tom Nebel who clearly saw the vision of Lean's application to the twenty-first-century church and encouraged us to proceed. Thanks to Neil Cole and Alan Hirsch who took the time to read portions of the manuscript and make invaluable suggestions to make it better.

Three men deserve special recognition. Dr. Andrew Parris is a Business Process Specialist at World Vision International. Dr. Don Pope is Chair of the Management at Abilene Christian University. Dr. P. Kent Smith is Professor of Ministry at Abilene Christian's Graduate School of Theology. Andrew and Don spent much of their careers implementing Lean in the aerospace industry. Before that they were at the Massachusetts Institute of Technology where they were part of the crew that kicked off Lean Enterprise in the U.S. In 2004, Christianity Today published a seminal article written by the three of them titled *The Lean Church: Streamlining Your Ministry for Maximum Effectiveness.* Andrew, Don, and Kent have served as indispensible advisors on the concept as well as the details of the book. They are remarkable men, all, and we are fortunate to have had them on the project.

Thanks to Best Man Glenn Larsen of Pine City, Minnesota, one of the clearer thinkers of the postmodern and post-Christian age and the most dauntless man we know. We wish to thank Janet Nelson of South St. Paul, Minnesota, Senior Chief Machinist's Mate Randall Braddock of Hampton, Virginia, and Joe Moleski of Orlando, Florida, for their incurable optimism and encouragement. We are also so grateful for the quality editing services provided by Erin (née Duffert) Desvousges of St. Paul, Minnesota ("Keep it simple, Dad!") and Maggie Flamingo of Madison, Wisconsin ("You have a destructive relationship with commas, Charles."). Their loving and supportive critique kept us between the white lines of English. Special thanks to Eric Johnson, previous Director of Latino Ministries for Converge Worldwide, and now a local pastor in strife-torn Monterrey, Mexico, for helping us not spin off into the far reaches of the theological cosmos.

And finally, thanks to the co-winners of *The Best Wife Ever* award—Kathleen Duffert and Betty Ann Hinds. They are indeed the best wives ever. God bless them for the godly women they are—they will both receive many crowns. If only we had the means to adequately reward them for who and what they are in this life.

Heartfelt thanks to all.

– Charles Duffert & Dr. Jeff Hinds
Wausau, Wisconsin

SOURCE MATERIAL

1. Barna, George. The Barna Group. Ventura, CA. www.barna.org.
2. Brickman, Leslie H. *Natural Church Development and Cell Church—Friends or Foes?* Longwood, FL: Xulon Press, 2005.
3. Burns, Ken. *The Civil War*. Arlington, VA: Public Broadcasting Service, 1990.
4. Cole, Neil. *Organic Church*. San Francisco, CA: Jossey-Bass, 2007.
5. Dennis, Pascal. *Lean Production Simplified*. New York, NY: Productivity Press, 2007.
6. Eldredge, John. *Wild at Heart*. Nashville, TN: Thomas Nelson, 2001.
7. Gingrich, Newt and Forstchen, William R. *Gettysburg: A Novel of the Civil War.* New York, NY: Thomas Dunne Books, 2003.
8. Gray, Stephen. *Planting Fast-Growing Churches*. Saint Charles, IL : ChurchSmart Resources, 2007.
9. Grenz, Stanley J. *A Primer on Postmodernism*. Grand Rapids, MI: Eerdmans, 1996.
10. Hirsch, Alan. *The Forgotten Ways*. Grand Rapids, MI: Brazos Press, 2006.
11. Hull, Bill. *Jesus Christ, Disciplemaker*. Grand Rapids, MI: Baker, 2004.
12. Kinnaman, David and Lyons, Gabe. *unChristian*. Grand Rapids, MI: Baker, 2007.
13. Kotter, John. P. *Leading Change.* Boston, MA: Harvard Business Publishing, 1996.
14. Lencioni, Patrick. *Death by Meeting*. San Francisco, CA: Jossey-Bass, 2004.
15. Nebel, Tom and Rohrmayer, Gary. *Church Planting Landmines*. Saint Charles, IL: ChurchSmart Resources, 2005.
16. Pascale, Richard, *Delivering Results.* Boston, MA: Harvard Business Publishing, 1990.
17. Powell, Colin, Gen. (U.S. Army–ret). *A Leadership Primer.* Loose PowerPoint Material. 1995.
18. Rainer, Thom S. and Geiger, Eric. *Simple Church*. Nashville, TN: Broadman and Holman, 2006.

19. Schwarz, Christian. *Natural Church Development.* Saint Charles, IL: ChurchSmart Resources, 1996.
20. U.S. Census Bureau. *Income Statistics, 2007.* http://www.census.gov/.
21. U.S. War Department. *U.S. Strategic Bombing Survey—Summary Report.* July 1, 1946. Washington, DC.
22. Warren, Rick. *The Purpose-Driven Church.* Grand Rapids, MI: Zondervan, 1995.
23. Willard, Dallas. *The Divine Conspiracy.* New York, NY: HarperOne, 1997.
24. Womack, James P. and Jones, Daniel T. *Lean Thinking.* New York, NY: Free Press, 1996, 2003.
25. World War II Multimedia Database, The. http://worldwar2database.com/.

ABOUT THE AUTHOR

Charles Duffert was born in 1947 in St. Paul, Minnesota and spent his formative years growing up on a dairy farm in Northwestern Wisconsin. Following graduation from the University of Minnesota in 1975 with a Bachelor of Science, he graduated the University of Nebraska in 1979 with a Master of Science, and then attended the University of St. Thomas 1988-1990 pursuing a Master of Manufacturing Systems Engineering degree.

Charles is now retired from his two varied and unusual careers – one spent in manufacturing leadership and consulting with the other as a U.S. Naval Officer assigned to the Navy's combat engineers, the Seabees. These careers were varied in that they allowed him to work in an extremely broad diversity of organizations and unusual in that both required significant national and international travel.

Although outwardly diverse, these careers had many commonalities and have developed in him some noteworthy characteristics. Among them: a passion for excellence and a disdain for waste; a talent for implementing lasting and improved change; and all have resulted in an improved process using applications of Lean- and Six Sigma-type improvements in real-world environments. He has been a change agent in more than thirty industries and is strongly persuaded that these methodologies can be used to implement change in the twenty-first-century evangelical church.

Charles and Kathleen, his wife of thirty years, have two daughters, a son, and two grandchildren—all of whom live in St. Paul, Minnesota. The couple lives in Wausau, Wisconsin. Charles' retirement interests include solo trekking in wilderness areas and finger-style guitar.

ABOUT DR. JEFFREY HINDS

Dr. Jeffrey Hinds was born in 1964 in Mechanicsburg, Pennsylvania, into a career U.S. Navy family. He and his two sisters were stationed with the family several places in the United States as well as abroad in the Philippine Islands.

At the age of twelve, Jeff was called by God to become a local pastor. He met and married his wife Betty Ann while they both attended Houghton College in New York State. Following Houghton he graduated Trinity Evangelical Divinity School as Master of Divinity and Dallas Theological Seminary as PhD.

He and Betty Ann have pastored churches in LaMarque, Texas, Dallas, Pennsylvania, and presently Wausau, Wisconsin. In mid-career, Jeff was offered a position as chair of the theology department at a Christian college. Instead, he accepted the position of Senior Pastor at Highland Community Church in Wausau—an opportunity to serve with an organization he felt matched his commitment to exegetical Bible teaching, a true desire to see people come to Christ, and contemporary worship styles.

He and Betty Ann have four children. Jeff's interests include church and family activities, sports of all kinds, and he continues to lead teaching trips to the Holy Land. His signature sermon is delivered annually on Reformation Sunday when he, dressed as Martin Luther in full period regalia, gives an account of how and why Protestants came to be. Jeff has traveled extensively, including to forty-nine of fifty U.S. States as well as to Europe, Africa, and Asia.